Founded in 1972, the Institute for Research on Public policy is an independent, national, nonprofit organization. Its mission is to improve public policy in Canada by promoting and contributing to a policy process that is more broadly based, informed and effective.

In pursuit of this mission, the IRPP

- identifies significant public-policy questions that will confront Canada in the longer term future, and undertakes independent research into these questions;
- promotes wide dissemination of key results from its own and other research activities;
- encourages non-partisan discussion and criticism of public policy issues by eliciting broad participation from all sectors and regions of Canadian society and linking research with processes of social learning and policy formation.

The IRPP's independence is assured by an endowment fund, to which federal and provincial governments and the private sector have contributed.

INSTITUTE FOR RESEARCH ON PUBLIC POLICY

iRPP

INSTITUT DE RECHERCHE EN POLITIQUES PUBLIQUES

Créé en 1972, l'Institut de recherche en politiques publiques est un organisme national et indépendant à but non lucratif.

L'IRPP a pour mission de favoriser le développement de la pensée politique au Canada par son appui et son apport à un processus élargi, plus éclairé et plus efficace d'élaboration et d'expression des politiques publiques.

Dans le cadre de cette mission, l'IRPP a pour mandat :

■ d'identifier les questions politiques auxquelles le Canada sera confronté dans l'avenir et d'entreprendre des recherches indépendantes à leur sujet;

■ de favoriser une large diffusion des résultats les plus importants de ses propres recherches et de celles des autres sur ces questions;

■ de promouvoir une analyse et une discussion objectives des questions politiques de manière à faire participer activement au débat public tous les secteurs de la société canadienne et toutes les régions du pays, et à rattacher la recherche à l'évolution sociale et à l'élaboration de politiques.

L'indépendance de l'IRPP est assurée par les revenus d'un fonds de dotation auquel ont souscrit les gouvernements fédéral et provinciaux, ainsi que le secteur privé.

INSTITUTE FOR RESEARCH ON PUBLIC POLICY

IRPP

INSTITUT DE RECHERCHE EN POLITIQUES PUBLIQUES

THE STATE OF EDUCATION IN CANADA

BY

THOMAS T. SCHWEITZER

AND

ROBERT K. CROCKER

GERALDINE GILLISS

STEPHEN T. EASTON, SERIES EDITOR

———

PART OF A SERIES OF MONOGRAPHS ON EDUCATION

PUBLISHED BY

THE INSTITUTE FOR RESEARCH ON PUBLIC POLICY

L'INSTITUT DE RECHERCHE EN POLITIQUES PUBLIQUES

Printed in Canada

Bibliothèque nationale du Québec
Dépôt légal 1995

Canadian Cataloguing in Publication Data

Schweitzer, Thomas T.
The state of education in Canada

(Monograph series on education ; 5)
Includes bibliographical references.
ISBN 0-88645-159-0

1. Education—Canada. I. Crocker, Robert K.
(Robert Kirby), 1940- II. Gilliss, Geraldine
III. Institute for Research on Public Policy. IV. Title.
V. Series

LA412.S38 1995   370'.971   C95-900985-X

Marye Ménard-Bos
Executive Director, IRPP

Copy Editing
Mathew Horsman

Editorial Assistant
Chantal Létourneau

Design and Production
Schumacher Design

Cover Illustration
Sylvie Deronzier

Published by
The Institute for Research on Public Policy (IRPP)
l'Institut de recherche en politiques publiques
1470 Peel Street, Suite 200
Montreal, Quebec H3A 1T1

Distributed by
Renouf Publishing Co. Ltd.
1294 Algoma Road
Ottawa, Ontario K1B 3W8
Tel.: 613-741-4333 Fax: 613-741-5439

The IRPP has commissioned a number of studies on topics in Canadian education, as part of its much expanded monograph series on public policy. The education series will include pertinent examinations of schooling from the very earliest ages through to the post-secondary level, and provide indepth analyses of various topics, including: financing, training and education and the importance of preschool learning.

Education is the cornerstone of our economic well-being, and in the current information age, characterized by rapidly evolving technologies, it has never had a more important role to play. The heart of our wealth is the knowledge and skills of our population. Our economic development, measured both domestically and against the success of our major trading partners internationally, depends to a great degree on our abilities to harness our human resources. In light of the importance of education in a fast-changing global context, it is not surprising that many of the assumptions of the past are being questioned. Does Canadian education measure up to world standards? Is it getting better or is it getting worse? Are Canadians getting good value for their money? The IRPP, in commissioning and publishing this series, seeks to provide some answers.

In the first monograph of this series, Edwin G. West proposed an income-contingent loan repayment plan to improve the financial footing of universities in Canada. In the second study, Peter Coleman addressed the question of educational quality, asking, "what makes a good school?" The third monograph, by Bruce Wilkinson, contained a call for greater public choice in education, to improve the efficiency and accountability of the school system. Stephen Lawton, author of the fourth work in the series, blames the bureaucratization of schools for the decline in the quality and effectiveness of Canadian education. He argues that the Charter School model is a potential remedy.

In the present volume, Thomas Schweitzer, formerly with the Economic Council and now an independent consultant, analyzes the relevant data on the performance of Canadian schools, offering a report card on where we are and a guide for where we should be heading. In his forthright discussion, he argues across crucial issues such as the reliability of testing, the "Effective School" model and the importance of home and community in promoting educational excellence.

Two eminent education specialists, Robert Crocker, Associate Deputy Minister of Education in Newfoundland, and Geraldine Gilliss, Director of Research and Information Services for the Canadian Teachers' Federation, critique Schweitzer's work, providing useful counterpoints and further clarification.

The ideas described here constitute an important contribution to the debate about the quality and effectiveness of Canada's school system. They must be addressed if we are to make real progress in safeguarding the future of our children. Finally, it should be noted that the opinions expressed in this study are the responsibility of the authors and do not necessarily reflect the views of IRPP or its Board of Directors.

Monique Jérôme-Forget, President
IRPP

CONTENTS

When Canadians ask "What kind of a report card should we give our schools?" it is difficult to get a clear answer. For most of us, evaluating our schools is an impossible task as we have little or no basis for comparison beyond our own experiences. Tom Schweitzer, a former Senior Economist with the Economic Council of Canada and now independent consultant on education, has produced a monograph to provide some benchmarks to make that job of comparing schools possible. He examines data from a number of sources to try to piece together a picture of the state of education in Canada today. And piece together he must. In contrast to performance measures available in many other countries, we in Canada do not evaluate the performance of our students across time and around the country in ways that make comparisons easy. As a result, when we see the kinds of differences in achievement that Schweitzer reports, we may be astounded. Where we live certainly seems to be linked to what kind of education our children will obtain.

Schweitzer begins by describing what contributes to a good education. The kinds of things that we might look for in our educational system include (among others) the degree to which students stay in school until they achieve some minimum level of proficiency, reach a level that will permit them to earn a living or to be able to acquire additional education or training, become good citizens and enrich their lives by exposure to the arts and literature of our cultures.

But many Canadian students do not reach these goals very well. Canada's educational establishment is not able to retain as many students at age 17 as a number of other developed countries. Further, there is at least some evidence that Canadians are becoming less satisfied with the perceived quality of their schools during the past decade. But how valid are these concerns? Schweitzer assembles the evidence of a dozen international studies in which there was at least some Canadian participation to argue that although our younger students tend to do well in comparison to other countries, by the end of high school they do less well. This is particularly the case in mathematics.

The comparisons across provinces are also significant. The range of variation among the provinces is striking. *At age 16 the average student in some systems is as much as six years ahead of the average student in other educational jurisdictions.* What an astonishing finding, to say the least! Surely such an observation is worthy of investigation and concern. Perhaps those of us in less successful provinces will ask our ministers of Education to explore, explain and offer remedies since other systems appear to do the job better.

And does the quality of schooling make a difference? Schweitzer points out that those students who have relatively strong numeracy and literacy skill scores earn a significant premium over those who do not. And since students in some regions are able to reach higher levels of achievement, this has ramifications for their lifetime income. If our schools really do make a difference, and we certainly spend a vast amount of money assuming that they do, then surely we have an obligation to encourage those practices that generate success and help those who are failing to improve.

So how do we achieve effective schooling? Schweitzer points to examples of programs around the world that have been successful. The important components of education — the family, the teacher and the schools — each receive some attention, as do curriculum and the design of our delivery systems. Are our teachers good enough? Are families sufficiently attentive? Are schools too bureaucratic? We have some way to go before we get the best performance out of our school systems. There is certainly room for improvement. Schweitzer has highlighted a number of ways in which we can see the difficulties. It is ironic that it is so difficult to write a report card for schools in the same way we insist that schools report to us. No problem was ever solved by ignoring the evidence. We have erred by neglect. We have not insisted on evaluating our systems of education around the country to see how well they are doing for our children. This book constitutes a beginning, in that it permits parents to see how well their child's peers are doing, in Canada and around the world.

In his response to Schweitzer's work, Robert Crocker, Associate Deputy Minister of Education in Newfoundland and professor of education, points to the strong revival in interest in educational assessment as a phenomenon of the 1980s and 1990s. Assessment has returned to education *via* the political agenda, and is forcing us to become more aware of our international surroundings. Sadly, however, he concludes that the evidence is too sparse to support many of the conclusions that Schweitzer has reached with much conviction. However, he too supports the idea that we must try to identify where we stand so that we can improve. It is just that we still do not have enough information to do the job properly. His belief, however, is "that it is doubtful if the high cost of education in Canada is justified by the results." But equally, insufficient attention has been paid to the organization of the school and the classroom as a mechanism for achieving better performance.

Crocker is optimistic about the future of Canadian education. Ever since the issue of achievement was placed on the political agenda, there has been a push toward increased accountability. Over the past five years, almost every province has begun to reassess education — even, at last, Ontario. And the suggested solutions are "surprisingly consistent": insist on higher standards; develop consistent measures of achievement; push for mechanisms that will lead to greater accountability on the part of those spending the money. Getting reform in education is a slow and frustrating task, but once started the same inertia that made for a sluggish response will tend to carry at least some reforms forward.

Geraldine Gilliss, the Director of Research and Information Services for the Canadian Teachers' Federation, finds that the evidence on Canadian performance is not as clear as Schweitzer seems to suggest. But just as importantly, she ascribes little importance to Schweitzer's claim that one of the roles of elementary and secondary education is to prepare a child to "earn a living." The more important goal from her perspective is that of developing the qualities of the individual. Thus it is no surprise that teachers are thought to be less successful in promoting the skills needed to earn a living *per se.*

Gilliss takes issue with Schweitzer's claim that the retention rate is relatively low in Canada, and that secondary school students do increasingly less well as their education progresses. Further, she argues, the explanation for the differing quality of the results among countries may be related to factors not directly part of the educational system. The curriculum may reflect social and economic conditions, and thus cross-country studies may not be very fruitful in reflecting a true comparison.

The quality of the teaching profession is very much an issue. Although it is true in the United States that teachers frequently have lower scores than many other professions on standardized tests, Gilliss claims that this is not the case in Canada. She argues that there is an excess demand for those wishing to go into teaching and this has resulted in increased requirements for teachers.

There are problems in our schools, but they perform well in general. The way to improve schooling is to work together with all the agencies in society, with a special emphasis on the family.

Schweitzer's response to these criticisms is frank and direct. The reader should enjoy the joust.

THE STATE OF EDUCATION IN CANADA

BY

THOMAS T. SCHWEITZER

I N T R O D U C T I O N

There is a growing disquiet about the state of education in Canada. Parents are dissatisfied with the quality of schooling their children receive and are organizing community groups to express their concern. Businessmen are complaining about the weak functional literacy and numeracy of the new entrants into the labour force. Taxpayers maintain that the school system does not deliver value for the money. Teachers emphasize that a variety of social problems, including lack of parental support of schooling, child poverty and new immigrant children's ignorance of the language of instruction, make teaching extraordinarily difficult. Universities are organizing tests and courses for first-year students who are unable to express themselves clearly and concisely in writing. Almost every year some province or other launches a royal commission or a committee of inquiry on aspects of educational policy. Since the early 1980s, Canadian provinces have increasingly participated in international studies of educational achievement. In December 1991, the Council of Ministers of Education launched the School Achievement Indicators Program (SAIP). Think-tanks publish monographs on education policy. No week goes by in the media without a report, article or letter to the editor on some aspect of the Canadian educational system. Is the concern justified, or is it merely a fashion, a passing fad? And if justified, what are the roots of the trouble? What can we do to improve the situation?

Although accurate information about the quality of Canadian education is difficult to piece together, in this monograph I attempt to do exactly that. Canadian education needs a clear and forthright appraisal. A frequent view is that there are difficulties in education and that they are getting worse. This is also strongly suggested by my review of the evidence. We are spending more than $25 billion a year on public primary and secondary education; we owe it to ourselves to scrutinize the performance of our schools. To do that job, we need to know how well our schools are doing, in what dimensions they are successful and in what ways they are failing. We need a report card on schools for exactly the same reasons we insist on a report card for each of our children.

In this monograph, I shall restrict myself to the discussion of primary and secondary education. This does not mean that I am belittling the importance of post-secondary education; rather, it indicates my conviction that education is a cumulative process. Dealing with universities and colleges without having first examined the lower levels of education is like being concerned about the top level of a building before ascertaining whether the foundations are sound. As for the nursery school and kindergarten, their importance is very great indeed; but attendance at that level is not compulsory in Canada, so I shall omit discussion of them in what follows.

To discuss the state of education in Canada, we must first deal with the question: what are the purposes of education? This is done in chapter two of the present monograph. Chapter three shows that primary and secondary education is easily accessible to all young Canadians, but not all are taking full advantage of this. *Accessibility* is very important, but of little use if the *quality* of education is questionable. Chapter four is a summary of the results of recent opinion polls regarding the quality of schooling. These polls reflect the subjective judgement of the people surveyed. More objective results are obtained in the international, interprovincial and intertemporal studies of student knowledge. These are discussed in chapter five, and they indicate that Canadian education is mediocre at best, and weak at the Grade 11-12 level. Also, they show that there are very wide differences in achievement among the Canadian provinces. These findings are based on test results. The validity of tests is questioned by many people inside and outside the educational fraternity. Chapter six discusses the pros and cons of testing, and concludes that *properly designed* tests are useful indicators of the quality of education.

Chapter seven describes in what way the students themselves, their families, teachers and school resources can influence the outcomes of the educational process. The practitioners of a particularly useful branch of the theory of education try to isolate the factors that result in effective schools. Their findings are summarized in chapter eight. The Effective School literature emphasizes the importance of the positive school spirit. However, in a system of compulsory and predominantly public education, the schools have to conform to educational policy directives set out by the school boards and departments of Education. Chapter nine contains a discussion of some current educational policy questions.

In recent years, we have witnessed an ever-increasing demand by parents that they choose the school for their children. In chapter ten, I point out the strengths and weaknesses of this movement. I conclude that some improvements could be made through freer school choice; but it is easy to exaggerate its advantages and it is not a universal panacea.

Chapter eleven shows that the characteristics of Canadian education are reflections of our society, and are, therefore, difficult to change quickly. Nevertheless, it is possible to change our system if there is a recognition of the need to change and if there is a will to do so.

A number of difficult questions in educational theory remain unanswered. Chapter twelve outlines a research program that would provide answers to these important questions and would help us to improve the educational system. In turn this would contribute to the prosperity of future generations of young Canadians.

The Purposes of Education

How good is the Canadian educational system? To answer this question, we must first consider the purpose of education. One possible reply is that the purpose of education is to prepare the pupils for their next phase(s) in life. But this answer is so general as to be vacuous. If we observe the infinite variety in the abilities, skills, tastes, interests, inclinations, career possibilities and life aims of young Canadians, it becomes obvious that we must be more specific. Over the centuries, educators, social scientists and philosophers have drawn up many lists of the aims of education, some shorter, some very long indeed. A leading contemporary American expert has enumerated 62 goals of education.[1] Such a long list may be self-defeating. However most people would probably be willing to agree to a shorter one containing the following items:

■ *Training for earning a living.* Many people would regard this as the most important goal of education, but even those who would regard it as too narrow an aim must admit it is an essential one. Note that this goal includes knowledge and skills and also good working habits. It implies the ability to think, reason and reach conclusions. Also, in this age of extraordinary rapid scientific and technological change and obsolescence, training for earning a living must include learning how to learn and acquire new needed knowledge.

■ *Training for further education.* Some 30 percent of our young people aged 18-21 proceed to post-secondary education.[2] For them, secondary education must provide the foundations for further study. As post-secondary education usually provides less direct supervision and control by the teaching staff than do primary and secondary education, good working habits and the ability to learn on one's own are vitally important here too.

■ *Good citizenship.* This has been acknowledged as a crucially important aim of education for millennia. It includes honesty, socialization, courtesy, acceptance and tolerance toward others and a peaceful resolution of conflicts. Many think that this should also include teaching virtue. However, as Aristotle pointed out some 2,300 years ago, "no one knows on what principle we should proceed...Again, about the means there is no agreement; for different persons, starting with different ideas about the nature of virtue, naturally disagree about the practice of it."[3] Aristotle's statement is as valid today as it was in his day. This is shown by the debates raging about the morality of genetic engineering, euthanasia, abortion, legalization of soft drugs and similar issues. *Except for the virtues mentioned at the beginning of this point*, schools would do wiser to avoid questions of morality and leave this controversial area to the family. The family can provide moral education, if it so wishes; but school-taught morality will be ineffective if not supported by the moral attitude of the home.

■ *Health and physical development.* This aim includes the elements of physical and mental hygiene. It has been regarded as one of the aims of education since classical antiquity.

■ *Richness of inner life.* This includes happiness, self-confidence, sense of self-worth and self-discipline. Some educators regard these as preconditions of educational achievement, others think that schooling can develop these qualities. The two views are not necessarily contradictory.

■ *Appreciation of the arts and philosophy.* These may not be of immediate practical usefulness, but beyond doubt enrich one's inner life. Music, in particular, has been part of the educated person's curriculum ever since classical Greece.

■ *Creativity and originality.* Many experts include this as a goal of education. Whether originality can be taught and learned is, however, an open question.

The very multiplicity of these goals of education raises difficult questions. For generations Canadians have lived in a country whose natural resources provided a high and rising standard of living. Changes in the world economy are rapidly changing our competitive position. The role and value of raw materials is declining compared to that of knowledge and skills ("human capital"). The relative position of our standard of living compared to that of other industrialized nations can be maintained in the future *only* if we have at least as well educated, trained and flexible a labour force as they. This is all the more important because the countries of the Pacific Rim have improved the quality of the education of their labour force tremendously, and most other industrialized countries are scrambling to keep pace.

Even if achievement in each goal enumerated above were quantifiable and measurable, how are we to compare them and weigh their relative importance? This is a relevant point when resources are limited and/or tradeoffs have to be made between, say, vocational and academic training, or between sport and the arts. Is more teaching of computer skills preferable if this comes at the price of less sex education? Is training in a second language more important than one in interpersonal relations? What is the right resource allotment between the sciences and the arts? These are valid questions and they could be multiplied almost without end.

I shall turn first to the question of the accessibility of education for young Canadians. I shall discuss the quality of Canadian education at some length later on.

NOTES

1. John I. Goodlad, *A Place Called School: Prospects for the Future* (New York: McGraw-Hill, 1984).
2. Organization for Economic Co-operation and Development, *Education at a Glance: OECD Indicators* (Paris: OECD, 1993), pp. 128-31.
3. Aristotle, *Politics and Poetics* (New York: Limited Editions Club, 1964), p. 268.

CHAPTER THREE

ACCESSIBILITY

The quality of education received by students is a very important indicator of the state of a country's educational system, but it is not the only important one. Excellent education for a tiny percentage of the relevant age groups would be just as unsatisfactory an outcome as a poor quality education for the broad mass of students. Are schools equally accessible to all young people irrespective of social origin, gender or ethnic background? What are the completion rates for the total population and for relevant sub-groups? How do we compare internationally, and do we show improvement compared to the past?

AVERAGE YEARS OF SCHOOLING

There are several ways of measuring the accessibility of education. One of these is the average years of schooling. In this respect Canada's educational system is one of the very best in the world. For the population aged 25-44, the age group in which formal schooling is generally completed for most people, the median years of schooling was 13.3 years in 1991. (The median is the number where there are as many people with more years of schooling as there are with fewer.) This represented an increase of 2.2 years over the previous two decades and a continuation of the long-term historical improvement witnessed by Canada's population (see Table 1).

As this table indicates, there is little gender difference in the number of school years completed. Females tend to have slightly less schooling than males.

The national average conceals big differences. For instance, in 1986, 45 percent of the on-reserve native Indian population of Canada had less than a Grade 9 education, while the corresponding figure for off-reserve native Indians was 24 percent, and for the rest of the Canadian population it was only 17 percent.

DROPPING OUT

Free primary and secondary education is available to every Canadian child. This does not mean, however, that all of them take the opportunity to complete high school. Some drop out as soon as they reach the legal school-leaving age, or even earlier; others continue, but with less and less enthusiasm, and do not obtain their graduation diploma. One would think that it is relatively easy to define and measure the high school retention rate and its complement, the drop-out rate, but it is not! Many studies have calculated the number of high school diploma recipients as a percentage of Grade 9 high school enrolment four years earlier (three years earlier in Quebec, where secondary schooling ends with Grade 11). On this basis Canada's so-called apparent drop-out rate was 32 percent in 1990-91.[1] However this method often misses those who drop out and later return to complete their studies. Students who skip a grade, or repeat one, may distort the results. Also, comparisons of the apparent drop-out rates over time can be misleading. For instance, in 1982-83, Newfoundland lengthened elementary-secondary schooling from 11 to 12 years. In the year of transition, there were no high school graduates in that province and the apparent drop-out rate became 100 percent. In 1987-88, the Ontario credit requirements were increased from 27 to 30. In consequence, the graduation rate declined appreciably, and the complementary apparent drop-out rate increased correspondingly. By 1989-90, it was almost back to the 1986-87 level, as many students caught up with the increased graduation requirements.

Table 1

Median Years of Schooling, Population Aged 25-44 Canada, 1941-1991

Year	Total	Male	Female
1941	7.7	7.5	7.9
1951	8.2	7.9	8.5
1961	8.9	8.7	9.1
1971	11.0	10.9	11.0
1976	12.1	12.2	12.0
1981	12.5	12.6	12.4
1986	12.8	12.9	12.7
1991	13.2	13.2	13.1

SOURCE: For years 1971-91, see Statistics Canada, *Education in Canada* (1992), No. 81-229; and Statistics Canada, *1991* Census; *Educational Attainment and School Attendance, The Nation* (1993), No. 93-328. For previous years: estimates are of the author.

In order to obtain an alternative view on drop-outs, Statistics Canada conducted a telephone survey between April and June 1991.[2] A sample of 9,460 youths aged 18 to 20 were contacted and asked whether they were still in school, had graduated or had left school before graduating. On the basis of this survey, Statistics Canada calculated that 23.7 percent of the 20 year-old cohort left school, for a time or permanently, before graduating; 28.0 percent of the males and 18.9 percent of the females. This result can be regarded as reasonably close to the one reported in the previous paragraph, if we keep in mind that the School Leavers Survey was based on self-reporting and that some respondents "may have considered themselves a graduate if they received a certificate after completing Grade 10." Of the 23.7 percent who left school before graduating, almost half (11.5 percent) returned to school. By the time of the survey, 71 percent of the 20 year-old males and 83 percent of the females reported themselves to have graduated.

It is interesting to note that only 14.9 percent of those 18-20 year-olds who dropped out at one time or another said that they did so because of problems with school work, while 30.7 percent gave "boredom" as the reason and another 26.9 percent "preferred work to school." More than 30 percent of the non-completers claimed that they were A or B students. However, over 40 percent of the male non-completers of graduation requirements and about 27 percent of the female ones reported failing one or more grades in elementary school. This suggests that their "boredom" or "preference of work to school" was due to having fallen so far behind that they saw no hope of catching up.

The schooling of native Indians has improved considerably over the past generation. Only three percent of on-reserve students remained enrolled continuously until the last grade of high school in 1960, but 44 percent did so in 1988.[3] Nevertheless, this still fell far short of the general school retention rate of the Canadian population (63.3 percent).

How well are we doing compared to other countries? This is not easy to answer, because the educational systems of countries differ considerably from each other. For example, the typical starting age for upper secondary education, as reported by the OECD for 1991, ranges from 14 years in Austria, Italy, Spain and the United Kingdom to 16 in the Scandinavian countries and several others.[4] The duration of upper secondary education also varies among countries, from two to five years. A rough-and-ready but reasonable compromise may be to calculate the percentage of 17 year-olds who were enrolled in full-time upper secondary and post-secondary education.

Table 2 places Canada in ninth place among the 20 listed industrial nations. This is a mediocre showing, not an outstanding one; it leaves plenty of room for improvement. We must also keep in mind that our comparative showing depends not only on the enrolment rate, but also on the achievement performance of our students. For instance, Table 2 shows that a bigger percentage of 17 year-old Japanese youngsters is enrolled in secondary and tertiary education than that of 17 year-old Canadian ones. In addition, international studies of student achievement discussed in chapter five of this monograph reveal that Japanese students tend to score higher on achievement tests than Canadian students. This would further increase the advantage of Japan over Canada, beyond the one revealed by Table 2. Hungary also tends to score higher than Canada on such achievement tests: this reduces Canada's advantage over Hungary shown in Table 2.

The labour market outlook for drop-outs is poor. The unemployment rate for high school graduates was 9.5 percent in 1991, but 14.1 percent for drop-outs. A similar relationship holds true for most industrialized countries.[5] Those who had jobs were earning substantially less than secondary school graduates. In 1990, Canadian drop-outs aged 25-34 earned 23 percent less than graduates.[6] Sid Gilbert and his colleagues, discussing the results of the School Leavers Survey, conclude that those drop-outs who find jobs work very long hours and are very poorly paid. "The labour market and life prospects of leavers [i.e., drop-outs] appears to be dismal...In light of the long work hours, it may be difficult for leavers to escape from their economic and educational circumstances."[7] This is a very discouraging finding, particularly when we observe that drop-outs are much more likely to come from broken families or be children of parents with low schooling, blue-collar jobs and little appreciation of the importance of high school completion. Thus, low education and poverty tend to perpetuate themselves from generation to generation. In addition, the rate of soft drug use is almost twice as high and that of hard drugs more than three times as high among drop-outs than among graduates. The criminal conviction rate during the last year of school attendance is four times higher among the drop-outs than among the graduates.[8]

Table 2

Full Time Enrolment Rates in Upper Secondary and Tertiary Education at Age 17. Selected Countries, 1991

Country	Percent
Japan (senior secondary only)	88.8
Belgium	88.1
Sweden	85.3
Finland	85.2
Norway	84.7
France	83.3
Switzerland	82.0
German Federal Republic	81.6
Canada	**79.3**
United States	77.0
Denmark	73.4
Netherlands	72.0
Ireland	70.6
Spain	64.3
New Zealand	58.9
Hungary	49.3
Portugal	49.0
United Kingdom	44.3
Czech and Slovak Federal Republics	39.8
Turkey	31.9

SOURCE: Organization for Economic Co-operation and Development, *Education at a Glance: OECD Indicators* (Paris: OECD, 1993), pp. 206-08.

1. Sid Gilbert, L. Barr, W. Clark, M. Blue and D. Sunter, *Leaving School: Results from a National Survey Comparing School Leavers and High School Graduates 18 to 20 Years of Age* (Ottawa: Minister of Supply and Services, 1993).
2. Statistics Canada, *School Leavers Survey* (1991).
3. Economic Council of Canada, *A Lot to Learn: Education and Training in Canada* (Ottawa: Canada Communications Group, 1992).
4. Organization for Economic Co-operation and Development, *Education at a Glance: OECD Indicators* (Paris: OECD, 1993), pp. 128-31.
5. OECD, *Education at a Glance*, p.188.
6. OECD, *Education at a Glance*, p. 191.
7. Gilbert *et al.*, *Leaving School*, p. 55.
8. Gilbert *et al.*, *Leaving School*, p. 47.

CHAPTER FOUR

SURVEYS

Having briefly discussed some aspects of accessibility and the drop-out rate I shall now turn to the question of quality. Some people think that one can form a reliable opinion of the quality of our educational system by conducting public opinion surveys: if the public is satisfied with the quality of our schools, this would indicate that our schools are good. If, on the other hand, the public — who, after all, pays for the school system — does not like what it sees, then there is going to be a continuous tension between the public at large and the educational establishment.

There are at least two problems with judging the quality of the system by public opinion poll results. First, the respondents may be inconsistent in their opinions, or even outright wrong on factual issues. Second, the adult respondents may view the present system by comparing it with the memories of their own past schooling rather than with the qualities needed for making today's generation stand up to international competition.

These points can be illustrated by the findings of three opinion polls commissioned by the Canadian Education Association.[1] The sample size of these surveys varied between 1,200 and 2,000. In all three polls, the respondents claimed that schools have improved over the previous five years, or since the school days of the respondents. Nevertheless, when they were asked to "grade" the schools of their own area, it turned out that their opinion of the schools had deteriorated (Table 3). The two statements are evidently contradicting each other.

These opinion polls throw interesting light on the views of the Canadian public regarding our schools. Table 4 summarizes the satisfaction with the students' intellectual and human and social development. It shows that on the whole the public is satisfied with the outcomes of our educational system. It also shows where the perceived weaknesses are and it contains some curious inconsistencies.

The data of Table 4 also contain some interesting inconsistencies. For example, reading and writing being the indispensable pre-requisites to all further learning, it is surprising to see that the public is less satisfied with the scholastic development in these subjects than with that in math and science. Is this perhaps due to the possibility that the public had less schooling than the current generation, is itself weak in math and science and can therefore not judge the students' achievement properly?

Regarding the public's opinion of students' human and social development, it is odd to see that, according to the poll, students are showing more racial tolerance than tolerance in general toward others. Also, one would think that "sense of self-worth and confidence" would be rooted in "self-discipline and personal initiative." Nevertheless, the public gives students a lower score in the latter than in the former.

The 1990 poll also asked those people surveyed to assign grades to the schools of their own communities. The findings are presented in Table 5.

It is noteworthy in Table 5 that, while the grade B is in almost all cases the most prevalent, the sum of the Cs, Ds and Fs by far outnumber the As. It is also interesting to see that, in the opinion of the public, schools are doing a better job in preparing students for post-secondary education than for a working life. This is particularly relevant for the 60-70 percent of the student body that does not proceed to college or university, but is entering the work force right away. It is also interesting to see that the public is reasonably satisfied with the preparation of girls in mathematics or science, even though specific studies investigating scholastic achievement show that girls tend to do worse than boys in these subjects. How should one interpret this poll finding? Are Canadians satisfied with the lower performance of the girls? Do they

Table 3

Grade Assigned by the Surveyed Persons to the Quality of Schools in their Area (percentage of respondents)

Year of survey	A	B	C	D	Fail	Do not know
1979	18.9	40.0	25.3	6.0	3.6	6.3
1984	10.0	38.2	26.7	5.0	3.3	16.8
1990	6.2	39.2	34.5	7.1	3.8	9.3

SOURCE: CEA Task Force on Public Canadian Education Association, *Results of a Gallup Poll of Public Opinion* (Toronto: Canadian Education Association, 1979); George E. Flower, *Speaking Out: Results of a Poll Conducted March/April 1984* (Toronto: Canadian Education Association, 1984); and Tom R. Williams and Holly Millinoff, *Canada's Schools: Report Card for the 1990s: A CEA Opinion Poll* (Toronto: Canadian Education Association, 1990).

Table 4

Satisfaction with Students' Development, Canada, 1990
(percentage of surveyed persons)

Development in	Satisfied	Neither satisfied, nor dissatisfied	Dissatisfied
Math, science, technology	67.9	12.1	20.0
Reading, writing, speaking	58.5	7.3	34.2
Problem solving	62.6	12.1	25.2
Respect for lifelong learning	55.1	14.3	30.6
Tolerance, respect, cooperation	58.8	13.1	28.2
Self-worth, self-confidence	63.7	15.5	20.8
Personal initiative, self-discipline	54.1	16.1	29.8
Racial tolerance	67.0	13.4	19.7
Dealing with social issues	61.0	13.7	25.3

SOURCE: Tom R. Williams and Holly Millinoff, *Canada's Schools: Report Card for the 1990s: A CEA Opinion Poll* (Toronto: Canadian Education Association, 1990).

Table 5

Grades Assigned by the Surveyed
Persons to Their Communities' Schools, 1990
(percentage of surveyed persons)

	A	B	C	D	F	No opinion
Effectiveness of teaching staff	14.2	44.3	26.1	5.2	3.2	7.1
Responsiveness to parents	18.9	38.8	25.4	6.6	3.2	7.1
Preparation for working life	7.5	28.8	35.9	13.1	7.8	7.0
Preparation for post-secondary education	10.1	34.8	30.3	8.7	6.1	10.1
Preparation of girls for science/math	12.0	40.8	29.0	7.7	3.8	6.7

SOURCE: Tom R. Williams and Holly Millinoff, *Canada's Schools: Report Card for the 1990s: A CEA Opinion Poll* (Toronto: Canadian Education Association, 1990).

regard it as unavoidable under the present social circumstances? Are they poor judges of the teachers in this respect?

It is generally accepted that the educational achievement of the labour force has an important influence on productivity, and thereby on the Canadian standard of living. It is therefore reasonable to inquire into the opinions of business people regarding the quality of workers' education and basic skills. The Conference Board of Canada, in co-operation with the National Literacy Secretariat of the Secretary of State of Canada conducted such a survey in 1989. A random sample of 2,000 firms employing more than 50 people received the questionnaire and 626 firms employing 771,000 people provided usable returns. An analysis of the survey yielded, among others, the following important findings.[2] Seventy percent of the responding firms maintained that they have significant problems with functional illiteracy in their organization and estimate that it affects, on the average, 10.7 percent of their work force This number is all the more disturbing because most of these corporations prescreen their job applicants before hiring, usually by demanding some secondary education or high school graduation as a minimum hiring requirement. At the same time, in the opinion of many enterprises, the number of years of schooling, or even the graduation diploma, is not a reliable indicator of literacy and numeracy skills. Forty-four percent of the respondents felt that there is a significant variation of skills for any given grade level. The extent of some unfavourable consequences of functional illiteracy are summarized in Table 6.

What conclusions can we draw from these survey results? The general public certainly does not give a thundering vote of confidence in our schools. In particular, it does not think our schools prepare our children well for a working life. Also, one third of the respondents think the reading and writing ability of our children is too weak. This squares with the findings of polls of business people.

Opinion polls have their uses. They can give information on subjects that are difficult to quantify. Also, they can be useful for policy makers who want to know about the wishes of, and ways of satisfying, their electorate. But they have drawbacks as well. Opinions are, by their very nature, subjective. They may be inconsistent or self-contradictory. Their best use is as supplement to, and complement of, objective quantified data observations.

Table 6

Impact of Illiteracy on Selected Business Issues Canada, 1989 (percentage of surveyed establishments)

Productivity losses	30
Input or process errors	40
Lower product quality	27
Problems with employee promotion	40

SOURCE: Robert C. DesLauriers, *The Impact of Employee Illiteracy on Canadian Business* (Ottawa: The Conference Board of Canada, Report 58-90-E, 1990).

NOTES

1. Tom R. Williams and Holly Millinoff, *Canada's Schools: Report Card for the 1990s: A CEA Opinion Poll* (Toronto: Canadian Education Association, 1990); George E. Flower, *Speaking Out: Results of a Poll Conducted March/April 1984* (Toronto: Canadian Education Association, 1984); and CEA Task Force on Public Canadian Education Association, *Results of a Gallup Poll of Public Opinion* (Toronto: Canadian Education Association, 1979).
2. Robert C. DesLauriers, *The Impact of Employee Illiteracy on Canadian Business* (Ottawa: The Conference Board of Canada, Report 58-90-E, 1990).

OBJECTIVE MEASURES

INTERNATIONAL COMPARISONS

In view of the supposed widespread interest in the quality of Canadian education there is a surprising scarcity of objective quantitative information on the subject. Of course, many of the criteria of a good education enumerated on the preceding pages are difficult or even impossible to quantify. I am thinking, in particular, of originality and creativity. But even where quantification is possible, as in the case of juvenile delinquency, provinces tend to have differing criteria and reporting practices, and this renders comparisons over time and among provinces extremely difficult. *There are no consistent country-wide data available on school absenteeism or on discipline problems.* Even in the field of cognitive achievement (that is, what do the students know?) the information is so fragmentary and widely dispersed that any attempt to form a coherent view is like trying to assemble a mosaic picture from a heap of individual glass cubes. Fortunately, it can be done by bringing together the results of international and interprovincial studies of tests in which Canadian provinces participated. The *cumulative* effect of the evidence is persuasive. However, the accumulation and evaluation of this evidence are made difficult by the fact that education is in Canada a jealously guarded provincial responsibility; and, unlike some other federal states (for instance the United States), we have no federal Department of Education. Also, participation in such studies is voluntary. For instance, *no* Canadian province participated in the First International Study of the International Association for the Evaluation of Educational Achievement (IAE) that took place in the mid-1960s, and *only two* provinces (British Columbia and Ontario) participated in the Second International Mathematical Study in 1980-82. In subsequent international studies the number of Canadian participating provinces varied.

In the following discussion I shall report the average outcome of the participating Canadian provinces as compared to other participating industrialized countries. Many developing countries also participated in some of the quoted studies, but I shall omit them from the tabulations, because it is the industrialized countries that have standards of living and spending powers comparable to Canada's that are our main economic competitors. Due to the varying educational systems of the participating countries it was sometimes necessary to adjust the raw scores in order to compensate for the differences in years of schooling, drop-out rates, and for the fact that in some countries the taking of the subjects in question is not compulsory in the last year of high school. In Table 7, I have adjusted the raw scores for these factors.[1]

This table summarizes Canada's performance in several international studies. For example, the first column of row 3 indicates that the age of the students participating in that particular study was 10 years. The second column indicates that the test was administered in 1983-86. (The date varied from country to country.) The third column shows that the subject of the test was Science. The fourth column gives the number of participating industrialized countries (in this instance 14). The fifth column indicates that, in this instance, all 10 Canadian provinces participated in the international study; the sixth column shows that Canada ranked sixth. The seventh column reports that the US ranked in the eighth position and the final column shows that in this study Japan and Korea ranked highest.

Table 7 contains several interesting findings. It shows that:
- On the whole, Canadian students of the younger age groups (ages nine-14) tend to do better in international comparisons than do those at the end of high school.

Table 7

Canada's Performance in International Educational Studies

Age of students	Year of test	Subject	Number of participating countries	Number of participating provinces	Canada's ranking	USA's ranking	First in ranking
9	1990-91	Mathematics	10	4	8	9	Korea
9	1990-91	Science	10	4	4	3	Korea
10	1983-86	Science	14	10	6	8	Japan, Korea
13	1980-82	Mathematics	14	2	6	12	Japan
13	1988	Mathematics	6	4	2	6	Korea
13	1990-91	Mathematics	14	9	9	14	Korea
13	1988	Science	6	4	3	5	Korea
13	1990-91	Science	14	9	9	13	Korea
13	1990-91	Geography	9	8	3	5	Hungary
14	1983-86	Science	15	10	5	13	Hungary
18	1980-82	Mathematics	12	2	10	12	Japan
18	1983-86	Science	13	10	10	12	Hong Kong

SOURCE: Thomas T. Schweitzer, *International and Interprovincial Comparisons of Student Cognitive Achievement,* Working Paper No. 39 (Ottawa: Economic Council of Canada, 1992); and Stephen Lazer, *Learning about the World* (Princeton: Educational Testing Service, 1992).

■ Even the results of the students of these younger age groups are very mixed. For instance our students aged 13 placed second out of six in Mathematics in 1988, (row 5), but those aged nine only eighth out of 10 in 1990-91 (row 1).

■ By the end of high school Canadian students are, on the average, weak by international standards: 10th out of 12 in Mathematics; 10th out of 13 in Science.

■ On the whole, age group by age group, and subject by subject, Canadian students tended to do relatively better in the 1980s than in the 1990s. For instance, in Mathematics, those aged 13 placed sixth out of 14 in 1980-82, and second out of six in 1988, but ninth out of 14 in 1990-91. Similarly, in Science, the same age group placed third out of six in 1988, but ninth out of 14 in 1990-91.

■ The American system, which many Canadians are using as the yardstick for evaluating everything Canadian, is doing very poorly by international standards. It is not a useful yardstick in the field of education. In nine of the 12 studies reported in Table 7 the US scored in the bottom third, and was last or next-to-last in six studies.

■ The far-eastern industrialized countries tend to lead in most international studies of educational achievement. They placed first in 10 of the 12 studies reported above. Numerous studies show that North America could learn valuable lessons from the parental and student attitudes and teachers' pedagogic methods of these countries.[2]

■ Even though space considerations prevent presenting the detailed results of the other industrialized countries that partici- pated in the studies reported in Table 7, an extensive analysis of international studies shows that many European countries tend to do consistently better than Canada.[3] Examples are Finland, Sweden, Switzerland and Hungary. The industrialized countries of the Far East follow an educational practice that includes an intensive training lasting many years, preparing the students for the "examination hell" of the university entrance exams. This approach is now under attack even on its home ground, and even Japan is trying to mitigate it.[4] The Japanese approach to high school education would not be acceptable or desirable in Canada.

However, a study of the successful European systems may well repay the effort, because following established best practice is the simplest and least expensive way to improve.

INTERPROVINCIAL COMPARISONS

According to some political scientists, the federal system has the advantage that our provinces act as 10 laboratories of political experiment and can thus learn from one another. It is therefore a source of sardonic amusement to observe that until the early 1980s no use was made of this opportunity, and there were no valid ways to compare the educational achievement of the various Canadian provinces. Only when the provinces began to participate (as separate individual entities) in the international studies referred to in Table 7 did it become possible to find out whether their achievements differed, how big the differences were and whether they showed any systematic regularities.

Charts 1 and 2 show interesting and important contrasts and similarities.[5] Chart 1 gives the results of the second International Assessment of Educational Progress for 13 year-old students in mathematics.[6] In this study the authors report the average percentage of correct answers given by each country's participants. Chart 1 shows the deviations from the international mean. For instance the strongest participating country (Korea) scored 9.3 percentage points *higher* than the international mean of 64.1 percent. All countries scoring higher than the average show up as bars to the right of the vertical line at zero. On the other hand the countries scoring lower than the average show up as bars to the left of the zero line. The US, the weakest country, scored 8.8 percentage points *lower* than the international mean. It follows that the difference between the strongest and the weakest country is 18.1 percentage points. The Canadian achievement is *below* the international average and much below that of the leading countries.

All Canadian provinces except Prince Edward Island participated in this study. The provincial results are shown in Chart 2. This shows that the difference between the strongest participating Canadian system (Quebec French) and the weakest one (Ontario French) is almost as big as the biggest *international* difference: 14.2 percentage points *versus* 18.1! These very substantial interprovincial differences in educational achievement are not an isolated instance. Also, as I show elsewhere,[7] on the whole the west-

Chart 1

Second International Assessment of Educational Progress, 1990-1991 Mathematics, Age 13

Average Percent Correct
Deviation from International Mean (64.1), by Country

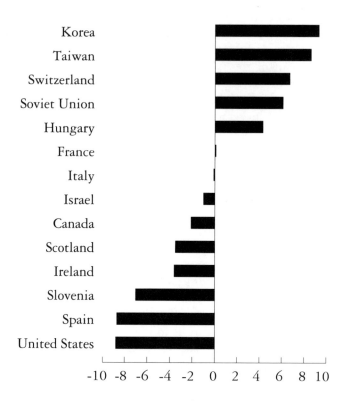

SOURCE: Archie E. Lapointe, Nancy A. Mead and Janice Askew, *Learning Mathematics* (Princeton, NJ: Educational Testing Service, 1992).

Chart 2

Second International Assessment of Educational Progress, 1990-1991 Mathematics, Age 13

Average Percent Correct, Deviation from International Mean (64.1), by Province and Language of Instruction

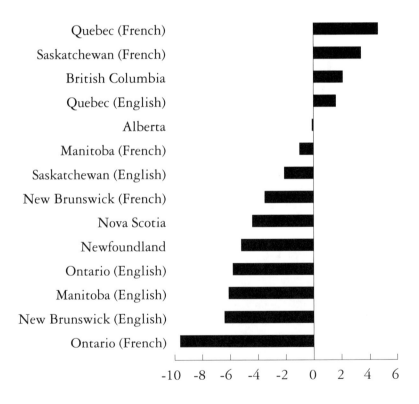

SOURCE: Archie E. Lapointe, Nancy A. Mead and Janice Askew, *Learning Mathematics* (Princeton, NJ: Educational Testing Service, 1992).

ern provinces tend to do better than the central provinces, which, in turn, usually do better than the eastern ones, just as they do in Chart 2.

The widely reported outcomes of the international studies stimulated sufficient public interest to induce the Council of Ministers of Education in Canada to inaugurate a School Achievement Indicators Program (SAIP). In April 1993, a set of mathematics tests was administered to random samples of 13 and 16 year-old students in all provinces and territories except Saskatchewan, which refused to participate. In this program, the scoring system differs from the one used in Charts 1 and 2. Each question was classified according to difficulty (level 1 for the easiest questions, up to level 5 for the most difficult ones). The students were assigned a given level of accomplishment if they answered correctly 60 percent of the questions of that difficulty level. I assigned level zero to those students who did not reach level 1, and also to those who were exempted from the test because they were identified by the teacher as not capable of satisfying the criteria for level 1. The Canadian average level of achievement in mathematics problem solving was 1.61 for 13 year-olds and 1.94 for 16 year-olds, resulting in an average annual progress of 0.11. Chart 3 shows the deviation from the national mean for each of the participating systems at age 16. This chart permits extremely interesting comparisons. For example, it shows that the strongest system in mathematical problem solving (Quebec French) is *almost six years* ahead of the weakest one (Northwest Territories). The Quebec French students are more than 1 1/2 years ahead of their Ontario English counterparts, who, in turn, are more than 2 1/2 years ahead of the Ontario French students. It will be very interesting to see whether the corresponding test in reading and writing, which was administered in the spring of 1994 and is in the process of being evaluated, will confirm the wide interprovincial differences shown in mathematics. The Council of Ministers of Education is planning a test in Science for 1996 and intends to repeat the whole cycle in 1997-1999. This will enable us to make valid comparisons over time as well.

The results for students were confirmed for the populations as a whole (not only for the student populations) by the Southam Literacy Study,[8] the 1989 Statistics Canada Survey of the Literacy Skills Used in Daily Activities[9] and the University of Calgary 1990 Survey of Scientific Literacy.[10] Furthermore, as far as school performance is concerned, we find that, since 1988, Quebec tends to do consistently better than

Chart 3

School Achievement Indicators Program, Mathematics, 1993
Problem Solving, Age 16
Average Level Achieved, Deviation from National Mean (1.94), by Province and Language of Instruction

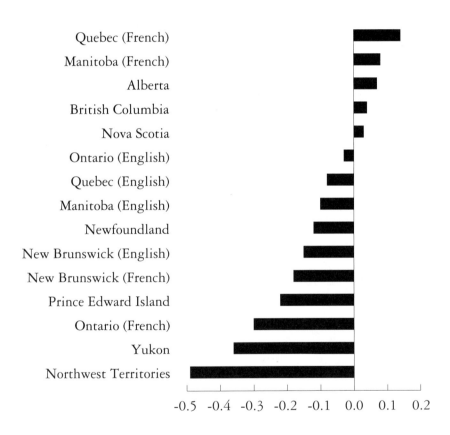

SOURCE: School Achievement Indicators Program (SAIP), *Report on Mathematics Assessment* (Toronto: Council of Ministers of Education, 1993).

Ontario. This is all the more remarkable, because Ontario has been historically more prosperous than Quebec (with a higher per-capita Real Provincial Product) and also spent more on education per student than did Quebec. While the performance of Ontario's English schools is poor, that of its French ones is even worse.

Does this difference in the quality of schooling really matter? It does, indeed! An analysis of the Statistics Canada Survey of Literacy Skills Used in Daily Activities shows that functional literacy and numeracy skills depend heavily on the quantity and quality of schooling.[11] In turn, income depends heavily on these skills. In 1988, the average personal income of Canadian-born males aged 16-64 was $26,417, and that of the corresponding females was $14,042. After adjustment for age, the average personal income of those males who scored in the top 25 percent for functional literacy and numeracy skills was about $14,900 higher than of those who scored in the bottom 25 percent for those skills. The corresponding difference for females was $10,200. Men scoring at the top 25 percent of the functional literacy/numeracy scale had, on the average, about 80 percent more income than those scoring at the bottom 25 percent. The corresponding income difference for women was more than 110 percent.

People with high literacy/numeracy skills had higher incomes because they were more likely to have and to hold on to jobs, and to be employed in well-paying occupations. This, however, accounts only for about half of the income differential. Even if we adjust for age, employment and occupational differences, those who score high on the functional literacy/numeracy scale earn substantially more than the low scorers.

INTERTEMPORAL COMPARISONS

There exist currently only two sets of data that permit valid comparisons over time. The Canadian Test of Basic Skills[12] has been administered to a representative sample of anglophone students in Grades 4 and 8 in the years 1966, 1973, 1980 and 1991. The tests cover Vocabulary, Reading Comprehension, Language Skills and Mathematics; a Composite Score is also reported. These tests indicate there occurred a substantial deterioration between 1967 and 1973. This was followed by a minor improvement between 1973 and 1980, but almost all of this gain was again lost between 1980 and 1991. In consequence, the 1991 performance was well below that of 1967.[13] The 1989 Statistics Canada Survey of Literacy Skills Used in Daily Activities also suggests that there has been a deterioration in the recent decades. After adjustment for years of schooling received, 16-24 year-old Canadian-born people (who were born between 1965 and 1973, and started school between 1971 and 1979), were doing worse in functional literacy and numeracy than the 35-44 year-old group (who were born between 1945 and 1954, and started school between 1951 and 1960). We have no reason to believe that our schools have improved during the postwar period, and it may well be true that they have deteriorated.

CONCLUSIONS ABOUT COGNITIVE ACHIEVEMENT

The cognitive achievement of Canadian students is mediocre at best and there seems to be no improvement over time. This is worrisome in itself, but it is made worse by the fact that Canadian education does not provide good preparation for the working life of those students who are not academically inclined. Many leading European countries retain only 25-50 percent of their 16 year-olds in general education, but they have for the others good and prestigious apprenticeship programs in a multitude of professions, often combined with formal part-time theoretical instruction. These programs can lead ambitious youngsters to further education, even to universities. In Canada, apprenticeship has little prestige, there is little of it available to young people and is often entered upon as a last resort, when other means of earning a living have failed.[14]

By trying to be all things to all students, the North American education system can be said to fall between two stools: it neither stretches the academically inclined as far as they could go and as far as the best foreign school systems do, nor does it equip the more practically inclined with the needed knowledge and skills to earn a living. Furthermore, it fails in a way that is both time- and resource-consuming. Japanese high-school graduates are said to be some four years ahead of their American counterparts in cognitive achievement.[15] The typical German apprentice is 17 years old. The typical Canadian one is 26.[16] Because we acquire the needed knowledge and skills slower than do the young people of our main competitors, the life-time productivity and standard of living of Canadians is necessarily impaired.

1. Thomas T. Schweitzer, *International and Interprovincial Comparisons of Student Cognitive Achievement,* Working Paper No. 39 (Ottawa: Economic Council of Canada,1992).

2. Thomas P. Rohlen, *Japan's High Schools* (Berkeley, CA: University of California Press, 1983); Harold W. Stevenson and James W. Stigler, *The Learning Gap: Why Our Schools Are Failing and What We Can Learn From Japanese and Chinese Education* (New York: Summit Books, 1992); and Merry White, *The Japanese Educational Challenge: A Commitment to Children* (New York: The Free Press, 1987).

3. Schweitzer, *International and Interprovincial Comparisons.*

4. Kazuo Ishizaka, *School Education in Japan* (Tokyo: International Society for Educational Information Inc., 1989); and Yasushi Tokutake, *Education in Japan,* About Japan Series No. 8 (Tokyo: Foreign Press Center, 1988).

5. They are based on a detailed analysis contained in Schweitzer, *International and Interprovincial Comparisons.*

6. Archie E. Lapointe, Nancy A. Mead and Janice Askew, *Learning Mathematics* (Princeton, NJ: Educational Testing Service, 1992).

7. Schweitzer, *International and Interprovincial Comparisons.*

8. Southam News, *Literacy in Canada: A Research Report* (Ottawa: mimeo, 1987).

9. Analyzed in Thomas T. Schweitzer, *Schooling and the Statistics Canada Survey of Literacy Skills Used in Daily Activities,* Working Paper No. 36 (Ottawa: Economic Council,1992).

10. Edna F. Einsiedel, *Scientific Literacy: A Survey of Adult Canadians* (Calgary: University of Calgary, mimeo, 1990).

11. Schweitzer, *Schooling and the Statistics Canada Survey.*

12. Nelson Canada, *Canadian Tests of Basic Skills: Manual for Administrators, Supervisors and Counsellors* (Scarborough, ON: Nelson Canada, 1990); and Nelson Canada, *Canadian Tests of Basic Skills: Forms 5 and Forms 7 Equating Study* (Ottawa: Report to the Economic Council of Canada, 1991).

13. Thomas Schweitzer, "The Issue of Quality," in *Education and Training in Canada* (Ottawa: Canada Communications Group, 1992).
14. Economic Council of Canada, *A Lot to Learn: Education and Training in Canada* (Ottawa: Canada Communication Group, 1992); Patrice de Broucker, "Education and Training: An International Perspective," in *Education and Training in Canada*; and Keith Newton and Tom Siedule, "The Learning Continuum: Adult Education, Training and Apprenticeship in Canada," in *Education and Training in Canada*.
15. Rohlen, *Japan's High Schools*.
16. Economic Council of Canada, *A Lot to Learn*, p. 21.

CHAPTER SIX

DO TESTS MEASURE THE QUALITY OF EDUCATION?

Much of the preceding discussion is based on the outcomes of tests. Are tests valid instruments of educational achievement? Vigorous debate has raged around this question. While many educational experts are firmly convinced of the usefulness of tests (otherwise they would not have invested the tremendous amount of time and energy required to do the studies I have cited), others maintain that the effort is misdirected and the results are misleading and/or misused. Who is right? And what are tests, anyway? These questions deserve detailed discussion because most of our knowledge about the quality of our school system is based on test results, and also because such results can be valuable diagnostic tools of the effectiveness of teaching methods and of accountability in the education industry.

Tests are, essentially, sets of agreed upon examination questions. Their results can be reported in two ways: norm-referenced or criterion-referenced.

Norm-referenced tests tell us how well a student (class, school, province, country) scored relative to, say, the average student (or corresponding entity) at the time the test was devised. Norm-referenced tests do not tell us what the student actually knows, but they give the student's position relative to his or her cohort. Unless the results are careful-ly adjusted, successive norm-referenced tests do not tell us reliably whether there was an improvement in achievement over time, because the achievement of the reference group or person may itself have changed over time. The Canadian Test of Basic Skills, mentioned above, has been adjusted so as to make valid intertemporal comparisons possible. As we have seen, students in Canada did less well in 1991 than in 1967.

Criterion-referenced tests show whether the students have met the criterion of correctly answering certain specified questions. For instance, when we find that in the Second International Science Study the 14 year-old Hungarian students answered correctly 72.3 percent of the 30 inter-nationally agreed upon test questions, while the corresponding American students got 55.0 percent right, this is a criterion-referenced result. It enables us to make valid intertemporal comparisons (provided the same test or differing tests of the same degree of difficulty are administered repeatedly over time), and can also show the strengths and weaknesses of the tested people in particular subsets of a subject (e.g., geometry or calculus) or even in answering individual problems. Note the difference between the two types of referencing: in principle, it is not possible for everybody to be, say, second; but it may be possible for everybody to get, say, 88 percent of the questions right.

Often one hears the argument that the purposes of education go far beyond cognitive achievement; therefore tests cannot capture these purposes and are useless as indicators of the quality of education. Advocates of tests respond that the purposes of education are indeed much wider than the mere acquisition of knowledge and skills, but usually success in increasing cognitive achievement goes hand in hand with success in inculcating the other virtues. The famous study of Michael Rutter and his colleagues showed that, after appropriate adjustment for the cognitive achievement of the students at the begin-ning of the observation period and for the socio-economic background of their families, those schools that showed the biggest gain in scholas-tic success were doing best in keeping absenteeism low (an indicator of good working habits), had lower juvenile delinquency (an indicator of good citizenship) and had fewer discipline problems (a measure of good interpersonal relationships).[1]

Opponents of norm-referenced tests claim that, by ranking students, the tests reduce the self-confidence and motivation of those who score low. Also, by increasing the competitive spirit, the tests are said to instill wrong values in students. The defenders of the tests point out that, whether we like it or not, the students will have to make their way in a competitive world, and to send them into it unprepared is as irresponsible as to send an athlete to a competition without training. As for criterion-referenced tests, how can students, parents, teachers and policy makers know whether a gain in knowledge has been achieved, if it is not measured? To the often heard argument, "It is more important that my Johnny be happy at school than that he score two percentage points higher in mathematics," the adherents of testing reply: "Maybe if Johnny scored 12 points higher in mathematics, he would be happier at school."

Opponents of testing point out that student performance on the very same test may vary from day to day. This is quite true. Anybody can have an unusually bad or good day from time to time. Therefore nobody should be evaluated on the basis of one test only, but on the basis of a combination of tests and regular course work. In a class, or in bigger samples of students, those with good and bad days would tend to cancel out and the performance of the group as a whole would remain indicative of overall achievement.

Some teachers maintain that they know their students and their achievement sufficiently well so as not to need tests to evaluate them. This is a dangerous argument. Many teachers feel, rightly or wrongly, that they themselves will be evaluated on the basis of their students' achievement. Under such circumstances the teachers will, consciously or subconsciously, bias their student evaluations upward. This is borne out in the provinces which have province-wide examinations for high school graduation and where the final mark is a combination of the exam and the teacher's evaluation. A relevant example can be found in Alberta. Over the January 1984 to June 1990 period, 14 exams were administered for the Advanced High School Diploma in six courses, altogether 84 exams. In five of these, the average school-awarded mark was lower than the centrally evaluated examination mark, in two they were equal and in 77 the school-awarded mark was higher than the examination mark.[2] Clearly, the teachers' evaluation was more lenient than the examination marks.

Opponents of testing also use arguments such as "no one has ever grown taller as a result of being measured."[3] But if you want to find out what treatment makes people grow taller, you must measure them to verify the effectiveness of the treatment. The same applies to curriculum policies, teaching methods and classroom practices.

Many teachers fear that test results will be misused, in particular by being used to evaluate teachers' effectiveness. If Teacher A's students score 65 at the end of the school year, while Teacher B's students score 60, does this mean that A did a better job than B? Not necessarily. If A's class had scored 55 at the beginning of the school year, and B's 40, then A's improvement over the year was 10 points, but B's was 20. It is the change over the year, in the economist's terms the "value added," that is the true measure of improvement.[4] This means that testing at regular intervals is necessary to establish the criteria for evaluation, not just a "snapshot" of achievement at a particular moment.

Some people claim that testing is harmful because it leads to "teaching to the test." Is this really such a bad thing? Is not all teaching, including teaching at the highest levels of university, teaching to the test? Who would like to be flown by a pilot who did not pass the requisite examination? If tests are poorly designed or inappropriate, then let us design better ones rather than discard the idea of testing completely.

The same argument applies to the criticism that most tests consist of primitive multiple choice questions and these test only for lower-order skills. There is a grain of truth in this. Testing and test evaluation are laborious and time-consuming; therefore, many tests are designed so as to facilitate their evaluation and analysis by computers. However, the School Achievement Indicators Program of the Council of Ministers of Education, Canada[5] proves that it is possible to design tests that contain both multiple choice questions and problem solving. Also, note that, if Canadian students do poorly in international studies based on lower-order skills-testing multiple choice questions, they would, in all likelihood, do even worse on higher-order skills tests. In the School Achievement Indicators Program Mathematics Assessment, there was a high correlation between scores in knowledge of Mathematics Content, which was 60 percent multiple choice, and Problem Solving, which contained no multiple choice questions at all. However, the scores in Problem Solving were consistently lower than those in Mathematics Content. Note also that the notoriously demanding Japanese university entrance examinations are in multiple choice format.

Some discussants of the international studies pointed out that the curricula of the participating countries differ and that this would influence the outcomes. This is quite true, and it cannot be held against students that they do not know what they have not been taught. But even here the usefulness of the studies and their test questions is obvious. They demonstrate that the curricula of some countries are rich while those of others are "thin" and, also, where the shortfall occurs. For example, the Second International Mathematics Study showed that British Columbia was the only industrialized participant that did not teach calculus in the last year of high school. This has now been remedied.

On the basis of the foregoing discussion, I conclude that the arguments against the studies based on tests are not convincing. The evidence is very strong that Canada's education is mediocre at best, that there are very big interprovincial differences in educational achievement and that there has been no improvement, possibly even some deterioration, in achievement over the last quarter century.

NOTES

1   Michael Rutter, B. Maughan, P. Mortimore, J. Ouston and A. Smith, *Fifteen Thousand Hours: Secondary Schools and their Effect on Children* (Cambridge, MA: Harvard University Press, 1979).

2   M.A. Strembitsky, *Alberta Education Diploma Examination Results: June 1990* (Edmonton: Edmonton Public School Board, mimeo, 1990).

3   J.H. Cockcroft, *Mathematics Counts* (London: HMSO, 1982), quoted in S.J. Prais and Karin Wagner, "Schooling Standards in England and Germany: Some Summary Comparisons Bearing on Economic Performance," *National Institute Economic Review* (May 1985), pp. 53-76.

4   Erik Hanushek, "The Impact of Differential Expenditures on School Performance," *Educational Researcher*, Vol. 18, no. 4 (May 1989), pp. 45-51; and Erik Hanushek and Lori L. Taylor, "Alternative Assessment of the Performance of Schools: Measurement of State Variations in Achievement," *The Journal of Human Resources*, Vol. 25, no. 2 (Spring 1990), pp. 79-201.

5   School Achievement Indicators Program of the Council of Ministers of Education, *SAIP: School Achievement Indicators Program Report on Mathematics Assessment* (Toronto: Canada Council of Ministers of Education, 1993).

———

CHAPTER SEVEN

PROBLEM AREAS

The great French sociologist and educator Emile Durkheim pointed out that every educational system is a reflection of the society in which that system operates. This implies that each society's strengths and weaknesses will be reflected in its educational system. But each society is also an interrelation of innumerable forces and influences. A country's educational system is the outcome of the interaction of its students, their families, their peers, teachers, school principals, educational policy makers and the rest of society that surrounds the educational system. It follows that it is very unlikely that the weaknesses of a country's educational system has only one, easily corrigible, cause. The following discussion will demonstrate the truth of this statement.

STUDENTS

The purpose of teaching is to educate students. It is therefore reasonable to begin the discussion at this level. A few fundamental statements may be appropriate at this point.

Achievement requires effort.

Effort requires motivation.

Achievement feeds back on, and reinforces, motivation.

Young children cannot be expected to possess the judgement and motivation of mature people. Their motivation has to be instilled by adults, in particular by their families.

These statements are so simple as to sound banal, but they have implications that are to many parents surprising and far from obvious. One such implication is that, once a child has fallen behind, he or she would need extra motivation and effort to catch up with the rest of the class. Indeed, leading educational researchers have found that the scholastic achievement of students by the end of Grades 3 or 4 is a good indicator of their final educational achievement.[1] Once students tend to fall behind, they lose motivation, which causes them to fall even further behind, leading to a vicious circle.[2] As mentioned above, in the discussion of high school drop-outs, a good one-third of these failed one or more grades in elementary school. From this it follows that the greatest attention must be paid by parents and teachers to the achievement of the students in the early primary years; that necessary remedial action be taken as early as possible; and that the students' motivation and self-confidence be supported. This, however, requires that the curriculum be set out clearly and communicated to teachers and parents, and that the strength and weaknesses of the students be measured, evaluated and communicated to the parents.

It is desirable that with the progressive maturing of the students they become eventually self-motivated. This requires that students learn to enjoy surmounting difficulties; to recognize that scholastic and career goals are necessary, that these can be achieved by concentrated effort and that this is a strenuous but enjoyable process. A continuing support of this process by the family, teachers, schools, prospective employers and society in general is a prerequisite of the internalizing of motivation by the students.

Working to earn money is, unfortunately, a significant rival to school achievement. D. Friesen found that almost two-thirds of all high-school students worked at least some time to earn extra money outside the home during the school year.[3] According to A.J. King and colleagues,[4] only 13 percent of Ontario high-school students who work do so to support themselves, contribute to family finances or to save for future education or other future use. Eighty-five percent do so in order to have more spending money for immediate consumption. While a moderate amount of work for pay is not harmful, and can even be a sign of initiative on the part of the student, working more than 20 hours for pay during the school week has a noticeable detrimental effect on the educational achievement of both sexes. It is particularly pronounced in the case of males. Forty-nine percent of male drop-outs worked 20 hours or more in their final year of school, compared to 34 percent of high school graduates. As King and M.J. Peart point out, young people working more than 30 hours per week for pay "...become, in effect, part-time students."[5] It is therefore very important that parents, teachers and society in general persuade the youngsters that immediate satisfaction of consumption desires should be subordinated to long-term career plans.

While it is true that the current recession has lifted the unemployment rate even of workers with tertiary education to levels unprecedented in the post-Second World War period, the unemployment rate of those who completed high-school remains considerably below that of drop-outs; not to mention the fact that the completion of high school remains, in general, a precondition of post-secondary education. Unfortunately, the needed support of motivation is not always forthcoming from the family. This is particularly true in families where the parents themselves have had little formal education. Forty-five percent of the drop-outs analyzed by Gilbert and his colleagues reported that one or both of their parents had not graduated from high school, compared to 32 percent of the graduates.[6] Further supporting evidence comes from a study done for the Toronto Board of Education, which shows that 85 percent of 15 year-old Toronto secondary students of high socio-economic status families (with parental occupation reported as professional/high managerial) had accumulated eight or more high-school credits, but only 59 percent of the children of families of low socio-economic status (unskilled clerical and manual workers) succeeded in doing so.[7] (A credit represents a subject pursued daily for a year in the secondary schools.) Similarly, the authors of the study report that 94 percent of the students from high socio-economic background were enrolled in Advanced level programs, but only 60 percent of the children from low socio-economic background were. As for marks, within the Advanced program, 42 percent of the students from high socio-economic background scored over 70 percent in both English and Mathematics, while only 32 percent of the children from low socio-economic background did so. Thus, non-completion of high school and weaker scholastic achievement in general has a tendency to perpetuate itself from generation to generation, another example of a vicious circle.

THE FAMILY

The first, and perhaps one of the most important things a family can do to help and motivate a student to good scholastic achievement is proactive: reading to the child regularly and frequently, well before he or she approaches school- or even nursery-school age. The importance of this cannot be exaggerated. But the family can help foster scholastic success in many other ways as well.

The discouraging results of the effect of socio-economic status reported in the previous section on students should be read with caution. *There is no reason to believe that low socio-economic background irretrievably condemns a child to low scholastic achievement and early dropping out.* The atmosphere of the home in general, and its attitude toward schooling and scholastic achievement in particular, are the crucial factors. This is illustrated by the study of the Toronto Board of Education, whose authors found that among the 15 year-old Toronto high school students of Chinese and Korean origin, 89 percent were in Advanced course and 79 percent had accumulated eight or more credits, even though only 6.3 percent of them came from families of high socio-economic status. This shows that families who attach high importance to scholastic success and are supportive can surmount the handicap of social status.

How can the family contribute to the good educational achievement of the child? In spite of the cultural differences, Canadian parents can learn some valuable lessons from the behaviour of Japanese parents as described by Harold Stevenson and James Stigler.[8]

The first, and most important, contribution is to make clear to the child that the parents regard scholastic success as important. Parents should follow the progress of the child carefully and be in regular contact with the teachers to make sure that the student is not falling behind. Also, the parents' attitude should be that the curriculum can be mastered by proper effort, and that lack of success indicates lack of effort, not lack of inborn capacity.

Together with these psychological supports go the measures to make educational success physically possible. The typical Japanese child has a room, or at least a desk of his or her own for regular study and homework, and often the mother follows the curriculum in order to be able to correct the homework if necessary. Great care is taken to ensure that the child has the proper nourishment and sleep necessary for intensive study.

The greater stability of the Japanese family is an important contributor to educational achievement. The Toronto Board of Education study shows that 74 percent of the 15 year-old Toronto students from two-parent homes were enrolled in Advanced courses, but only 67 percent of students from broken homes were.[9] Sixty-nine percent of the students from two-parent homes accumulated eight or more credits in Grade 9, while only 56 percent of those from broken homes did so.

In the previous section, the harmful effect of the students' spending too much time on work for pay was mentioned. In addition, the unfavourable influence of television is now firmly established. The detailed research of the international studies summarized in Table 4 shows with great consistency that the more time spent by the students on television watching, the worse their achievement. The authors of the important study conducted in Canada under scientifically controlled circumstances concluded that "second graders...who grew up without TV were better readers than children who grew up with TV."[10] The situation is particularly critical in Grades 1 and 2, where fluent reading skills are supposed to be acquired. Less intelligent children are at particularly high risk. The researchers concluded that "it is important for parents and educators to ensure that children spend sufficient time practising reading to acquire fluency to the point of automatization." The researchers "...suspect that most children find watching television a more appealing alternative, and this may be especially true for children who are less competent." In addition to the harmful influence of television on the reading acquisition and reading habits of students, the authors found that it had unfavourable effects on other educational goals as well, namely on creativity and problem-solving, both in children and adults. "This may be due to the fact that television may develop a relatively short attention span and/or low frustration tolerance..." The situation may be particularly dangerous in the case of commercial television, which interrupts the program every seven minutes or so and thereby methodically trains children for a short attention span. Given these by now well-established results about the deleterious effect of too much television watching, parental control and rationing are strongly advisable. As a matter of fact, it may be necessary for parents themselves to limit their own television viewing because it is too much to expect children to concentrate on their study or homework while the set is on in the next room.

The most important help parents can give is persuading their children not to be satisfied with a "pass" mark, but to exert themselves to the best of their abilities. What we thought to be "good enough" is not good enough any longer: the rewards of international competition will accrue to the best.

TEACHERS

A study published by the OECD points out that teaching is labour, a craft, a profession and an art.[11] Like all work, it should be properly remunerated, and I shall return to this subject below, where I discuss school resources. But for a professional there is more to the rewards of work than mere financial compensation. It is also important that the work be appreciated and carry prestige. At first sight it seems that the teaching profession satisfies this requirement. Bernard Blishen and his colleagues[12] ranked 513 occupations on a socio-economic scale based essentially on income and education received; secondary teachers ranked 23rd from top, and elementary and kindergarten teachers 42nd: a very respectable showing. However, even here an important point emerges: the previous discussion emphasizes the crucial importance of achievement in the early school years and of the sensitivity and skill needed to develop in young people a desire for life-long learning. This is not reflected in the Blishen ranking.

High as the socio-economic ranking of the profession may be, for many teachers teaching is not their first career choice. Ruth Rees and her colleagues found that only 64 percent of male and 71 percent of female elementary school teachers regarded teaching as their first career choice.[13] At the secondary level the situation was even worse: the corresponding figures were 37 and 56 percent respectively. This is very disturbing. Clearly, very many of our teachers are not happy in their profession — a profession that makes extremely high demands on its practitioners and requires full-hearted devotion to the task. Teaching is a beautiful, vitally important, extremely onerous vocation that is prone to "burnout":

> We hear and read enough about teacher burnout to assume that
> many teachers suffer from it. The principals interviewed in this

study corroborate this assumption; a number of them told us that dealing with teachers showing signs of burnout is one of their major problems.[14]

Motivation and a sense of self-worth are inextricably intertwined, as teachers know all too well from observing their students.

Why do teachers think that they are not treated as professionals? They have considerable freedom to make decisions in the classroom, but much less at the school and school district level. A typical example is the survey of the Edmonton Public School District.[15] Among other questions, the teachers were asked whether they think they have adequate influence over decisions that affect them and their job. The answers are summarized in Table 8. Even at the elementary level teachers feel that they are not sufficiently influential on policy issues at the school level, and much less so on the district level. The dissatisfaction progressively increases among the teachers of the higher grades.

The decline of the social prestige of teaching in general, and of high-school teaching in particular, is not a special North American phenomenon.[16] In 1911, the school enrolment rate of 15 to 19 year-olds was 19 percent. By 1988 it was well above 70 percent. This in itself has reduced the prestige of the high school, and of those teaching in it. In addition the teacher/student ratio has increased as well, as I shall discuss in the section on school resources. This has further reduced the "select" nature of the profession, not only in Canada, but also in many other countries. But very important exceptions remain: teaching continues to be a very prestigious profession in Japan.

The poor self-image of the teaching profession can become a very dangerous thing. It may deter potentially good teachers from entering the profession, and may thus lower the quality of the teacher stock in the long run. This would, in turn, further lower the prestige of the profession, creating a vicious circle. Something like this is going on in the United States. Studies of the Scholastic Aptitude Test (SAT) scores show that, among 29 identified university major specialization areas, students registering in education are ranking 26th.[17]

The international studies which revealed the mediocre performance of Canadian students, had, rightly or wrongly, lowered the social prestige of the teaching profession. What the critics do not take properly into account is the fact that more and more problems that used to be

Table 8

Teachers' Perceptions of their Influence
on Education Policy Decisions
Edmonton Public School District, 1985-1990
(percentage of teachers replying "much" or "fairly much")

Grades	At School Level	At District Level
Kindergarten to Grade 6	73.1	28.2
Grades 7 to 9	60.0	22.2
Grades 10 to 12	47.5	17.2

SOURCE: Edmonton Public School District, *Attitude Survey Results*, mimeo, 1990.

regarded as the responsibilities of the family, the churches and of society in general are now loaded on the teachers. Teachers are not trained, and cannot be expected, to teach effectively children who are suffering from ills such as malnourishment, lack of sleep, excessive television watching, broken families, domestic violence, alcoholism or other drug abuse.[18] Teachers and schools are there to teach. Their attempts to deal with the other problems of society will be unsuccessful, and at the same time they will impair their chances of success in the field of their comparative advantage, namely education.

SCHOOL RESOURCES

Between the ages of six and 15, schooling is compulsory in Canada and more than 95 percent of the students go to public schools. Thus the demand for educational services is vested in the state and is of a quasi-monopolistic nature. Not surprisingly, the suppliers of educational services, the teachers, have organized themselves into strong unions. In such situations, where an industry is monopolized and market pressures are not operating directly, there is a tendency to pay less attention to costs and the quality of output than under more competitive circumstances.

In 1991, public spending on education in Canada was 6.7 percent of GDP, the second highest share of the twenty industrialized countries reported by the OECD. This is partly due to our, by international standards, very high enrolment in, and spending on, post-secondary education; but our expenditure on primary and secondary education is also among the highest.[19] Conventional wisdom maintains that high spending is an indicator of high quality, and that we can improve quality by increasing spending. In particular, many believe that higher teacher/pupil ratios, more educated teachers, more experienced teachers, better paid teachers, more expenditures per pupil, more administrative inputs and better school facilities are conducive to higher educational achievement. All these measures make education more expensive.

An extensive review of the literature by Eric Hanushek summarizes the results of 187 studies dealing with the effect of these input changes.[20] Note that not all studies included all the changes mentioned in the previous paragraph. Table 9 is adapted from Hanushek's findings. It shows that comparatively few studies give results that are statistically

Table 9

Effect of Input Increases
on Educational Achievement

Input	Number of studies	Favourable effect	Unfavourable effect
Teacher/pupil ratio	152	14	13
Teachers' education	113	8	5
Teachers' experience	140	40	10
Teachers' salary	69	11	4
Administrative inputs	61	7	1
Facilities	74	7	5
Expenditures/pupil	65	13	3

SOURCE: Erik Hanushek, "The Impact of Differential Expenditures on School Performance," *Educational Researcher*, Vol. 18, no. 4 (May 1989), pp. 45-51.

significant — that is, are stronger than one could expect on the basis of pure chance — and even these few give very mixed results: sometimes increased inputs result in weaker educational achievement. Let us look at each of the important categories in more detail.

TEACHER/PUPIL RATIO

A high teacher/pupil ratio means small class sizes. Conventional wisdom maintains that small classes are conducive to better education. There is something to this belief, even though the Canadian class size has dropped by about one third over the last 30 years without any noticeable improvement in educational achievement. Very small classes should permit the teacher to adapt the teaching method to the personality and the ability of the students. Also, it is easier to choose the members of small classes in such a manner as to make the class homogenous in educational achievement at the beginning of the school year. This is an important point if we recall that education is a cumulative process that builds on the previous knowledge of the pupil. Indeed, there can be no doubt that the most extreme case of a small class, namely the one-on-one method of tutorial teaching, is the most effective method, if the teacher is highly motivated, sensitive and knowledgeable. However, the method of tutorials, or even of very small classes, is not financially feasible in a system of compulsory general schooling.

What is the situation with bigger classes? A survey of about 170 studies finds that smaller classes result in better cognitive achievement, but the improvement is very small in the relevant range (20 to 40 students per class).[21] For instance, it would take a reduction of the class size by one third to one half to bring the average student to the 60th percentile (that is, to make the student achieve better, or as well as, 60 percent of the students in the bigger class). This in turn implies an increase in schooling costs of close to 50 to 100 percent, because smaller classes require not only more teachers, but also more classrooms. Thus, improving cognitive achievement through the reduction of class size is obviously an implausible proposition for the educational system as a whole.

Most of the studies reported in Table 9 show no positive relationship between cognitive achievement and small class size. There may be many reasons for this. In some instances, students with learning disabilities may be placed in small classes. Some of the most successful countries, particularly the Far Eastern ones, are well known for their big class sizes. Also, it may be that the minor favourable effect of the smaller classes is obscured by the major effect of some other, more important factor of cognitive success that was not investigated in the studies.

On the whole, there is little argument in favour of reduced class sizes within the limits practised in industrialized countries with compulsory public education. However there may be exceptions. I have already mentioned the case of students who have serious learning difficulties. Small classes may also be justified in subjects where students need continuous practice and immediate, individualized feedback from the teacher. Conversational capacity and correct accent and pronunciation in foreign languages are typical examples.

TEACHERS

Education. Teachers' salaries depend on their educational credentials and their seniority. The credentials do not specify in which subjects they have to be earned. For reasons I shall discuss presently, most teachers tend to earn additional educational credits in school administration. This has nothing to do with ability to teach better. It is not surprising that Table 9 shows practically no relationship between teachers' education and students' achievement, even though salary raises caused by teachers' acquiring additional credits are an important part of the cost increase of education.

Experience. Among the seven inputs listed in Table 9, teachers' experience shows the strongest positive relationship with students' achievement, but even here the relationship is not overwhelming. Learning by doing is probably effective in teaching, as it is in other occupations. But the causal relationship may also work the other way round. One would expect less good teachers to drop out of the profession earlier than the better ones; in this case better quality leads to more experience, rather than the other way round.

Salary. Canadian teachers are well paid, both by national standards (compared to other professions requiring similar levels of education) and by international ones.[22] However, the structure and the increases of teachers' remuneration are arranged in such a manner that they do not give inducement to good teaching. The entry level salaries are relatively high and the salary increase pattern is relatively flat compared to other occupations. Also, the salaries are based exclusively on the basis of the teachers' educational credentials and their years of service, *not* on the quality of teaching.

ADMINISTRATIVE INPUTS

There is a rapidly growing literature indicating that administrative interference with teaching and school organization has an unfavourable effect on student achievement.[23] A recent US study finds that the addition of one person to the administrative staff reduces student achievement by about as much as the addition of a teacher increases it.[24] These findings accord well with Table 9.

FACILITIES

It is well known that the highly successful Japanese schools are quite austere compared to the typical American or Canadian school. The study of Gary Anderson and his colleagues shows that higher capital outlays per student have no effect on student achievement — although they do increase student retention rates.[25] In other words, more expensive surroundings do attract and hold more students but do not make them learn more, nor make the teachers teach better.

EXPENDITURES PER STUDENT

Some 75 percent of all school-board expenditures are spent on teachers' and administrators' salaries and on capital assets.[26] Table 9 shows that none of these inputs has a consistent positive effect on educational achievement. It is therefore not surprising that the same is true for total expenditure per student. Canada is already spending more per student than the average OECD country, yet our cognitive achievement is no cause for satisfaction. We have no reason to believe that even more spending would cure our current shortcomings. It may be that the inputs listed in Table 9 do have positive effects on educational achievement, but the omission of some other, more powerful variable(s) from the analysis prevented the demonstration of such positive effects. In any case, the burden of the proof rests now on those who propose more spending.

1. Benjamin S. Bloom, *Human Characteristics and School Learning* (New York: McGraw-Hill, 1976).

2. Robert K. Crocker, *Motivation and School Achievement*, a paper prepared for the Economic Council of Canada (1991) (Unpublished).

3. D. Friesen, "Jobs and Money: The High-School Culture," *The Canadian Administrator*, Vol. 23, no. 4 (January 1984), pp. 1-5.

4. A.J.C. King, W. K. Warren, C. Michalski and M. J. Peart, *Improving Student Retention in Ontario Secondary Schools* (Toronto: Ontario Ministry of Education, 1988).

5. A.J.C. King and M. J. Peart, *The Good School* (Toronto: Ontario Secondary Teachers' Federation, 1990).

6. Sid Gilbert, L. Barr, W. Clark, M. Blue and D. Sunter, *Leaving School: Results from a National Survey Comparing School Leavers and High School Graduates 18 to 20 Years of Age* (Ottawa: Minister of Supply and Services, 1993).

7. Maisy Cheng, Gerry Tsuji, Maria Yau and Suzanne Ziegler, *The Every Secondary Student Survey, Fall 1987* (Toronto: Toronto Board of Education Research Services, 1989).

8. Harold W. Stevenson and James W. Stigler, *The Learning Gap: Why Our Schools Are Failing and What We Can Learn From Japanese and Chinese Education* (New York: Summit Books, 1992).

9. Cheng *et al.*, *The Every Secondary Student Survey*.

10. Tannis Macbeth Williams (ed.), *The Impact of Television: A Natural Experiment in Three Communities* (Orlando, FL: Academic Press, 1986).

11. Organization for Economic Co-operation and Development, *Schools and Quality: An International Report* (Paris: OECD, 1989).

12. Bernard R. Blishen, William K. Carroll and Catherine Moore, "The 1981 Socioeconomic Index for Occupations in Canada," *Canadian Review of Sociology and Anthropology*, Vol. 24, no. 4 (November 1987), pp. 468-88.

13. Ruth Rees, Wendy K. Warren, Beverley J. Coles and Marjorie Peart, *A Study of Recruitment of Ontario Teachers* (Kingston: Social Program

Evaluation Group, Queen's University, 1989).

14. A.J.C. King, W. K. Warren and M. J. Peart, *The Teaching Experience: A Profile of Ontario Secondary School Teachers* (Toronto: Ontario Secondary Teachers' Federation, 1988).

15. Edmonton Public School District, *Attitude Survey Results*, mimeo, 1990.

16. Jacques Lesourne, *Éducation et Société: Les défis de l'an 2000* (Paris: Édition La Découverte, 1988).

17. Stephen T. Easton, *Education in Canada: An Analysis of Elementary, Secondary and Vocational Schooling* (Vancouver: The Fraser Institute, 1988).

18. Bruce W. Wilkinson, *Educational Choice: Necessary But Not Sufficient* (Montreal: Institute for Research on Public Policy, 1995).

19. For earlier data on our public spending on primary and secondary education see Easton, *Education in Canada*.

20. Erik Hanushek, "The Impact of Differential Expenditures on School Performance," *Educational Researcher*, Vol. 18, no. 4 (May 1989), pp. 45-51.

21. Gene V. Glass, "Class Size," in Torsten Hulten and T. Nevill Postlethwaite (eds.), *The International Encyclopedia of Education: Research and Studies* (Oxford: Pergamon Press, 1985).

22. Kathryn McMullan, "The Economics of the Teaching Profession," in Keith Newton (ed.), *Education and Training in Canada: A Research Report* (Ottawa: Canada Communications Group Publishing, 1992).

23. John E. Chubb and Terry M. Moe, *Politics, Markets, and America's Schools* (Washington, DC: The Brookings Institution, 1990); and Jean-Luc Migue and Richard Marceau, *Le Monopole Public de l'Éducation: l'Économie Politique de la Mediocrite* (Sillery, QC: Presses de l'Université du Québec, 1989).

24. Gary M. Anderson, William F. Shugart II and Robert D. Tollison, "Educational Achievement and the Cost of Bureaucracy," *Journal of Economic Behaviour and Organization*, Vol. 15, no. 1 (January 1991), pp. 29-45.

25. Anderson *et al.*, "Educational Achievement."

26. Gilles Mcdougall, "The Cost and Funding of Education," Keith Newton (ed.), *Education and Training in Canada: A Research Report* (Ottawa: Canada Communications Group Publishing, 1992).

CHAPTER EIGHT

EFFECTIVE SCHOOLS

At this stage the reader may well ask: if increased resources do not ensure better education, what does? The answer comes from the effective school literature. It has been observed that certain schools do consistently better than others. The effective school literature tries to identify such schools and to detect whether they have certain features in common. In their path breaking English study, *Fifteen Thousand Hours*, Rutter and his colleagues investigated 12 inner city schools in London.[1] They found that, even after adjustment for the ability, knowledge and family socio-economic status of the students when they entered the school ("the quality of the intake"), some schools achieved consistently better results, not only in terms of final examination success, but also on the measures of lower drop-out rates, lower absenteeism, fewer discipline problems and lower juvenile delinquency. James Coleman and Thomas Hoffer reach similar conclusions for the US.[2]

These successful schools have a number of features in common. Not all effective schools will show all the characteristics discussed below, but all will have most of them; and their general effect gives these schools a common spirit or "ethos."[3] To understand this, it is necessary to regard schools as social organizations consisting of students, teachers, administrators and support staff, devoted to transmitting knowledge and skills to the students. As in all social organizations, success depends on the willing cooperation of all the participants; but we must remember that the leadership must come from the school staff, and in particular from the principal, because we cannot expect from the students as much maturity, knowledge, experience and self-discipline as one would expect from adults.

Effective schools place great emphasis on academic work and convey to students the importance of academic success. In general, a purposeful program of compulsory curriculum subjects is more effective in raising academic standards than a wide choice of electives. Effective schools set high targets for their students, but not so high ones as to render them unachievable for a large percentage of them. Targets set so high that, say, 40 percent of the student body cannot reach them would discourage rather than motivate.

In effective schools, a high proportion of the time is devoted to active teaching and studying — to "time on task" — and relatively little on administration, disciplining, setting up of equipment, distributing papers, public announcements and other such activities. Some critics blame the shortness of the North American school year for the unsatisfactory performance of the students in international studies. In fact, international studies show no relationship between the length of the school year and/or of the school day, and achievement.[4] Efficient use of the time is more important than increasing the time.

Researchers preparing the international studies investigated whether the material necessary to correctly answer each test question has been taught by the teachers of the participating students ("opportunity to learn"). Not surprisingly, the studies found a strong positive relationship between opportunity to learn and student achievement. In the Classroom Environment Study of the International Association for the Evaluation of Educational Achievement,[5] it was found that in each country there were classrooms that had an opportunity to learn the content associated with two to three times as many test questions as did other classrooms. This further emphasizes the importance of the efficient use of time.

Effective schools also regularly monitor the individual student's progress. One way of doing this is the regular setting and marking of homework. This provides feedback from the teacher to the student, acts as a diagnostic tool for the teacher, develops a sense of self-monitoring of progress in the student and promotes good working habits. Only in this way can students know what is expected from them, and whether they are meeting the expectations. Only in this way can they develop pride in achieving goals. In effective schools, very good work receives prompt praise, however praise is not devalued by bestowing it indiscriminately for minor achievement. There is no disparagement of weak performance, because it is an ineffective method for spurring students to better achievement.

Successful teaching is not possible if the school atmosphere is undisciplined, rowdy and raucous. Effective schools have clear and reasonable rules of student behaviour and these rules are fairly and consistently enforced. This is necessary to develop a proud school spirit in which the voluntary cooperation of the student body helps to prevent undesirable behaviour of individuals. Such an attitude is helped by giving students, on a rotating basis, responsibility for maintaining discipline and preventing vandalism.

Effective schools show a community spirit within the teaching staff. The cumulative nature of educational achievement necessitates a joint planning of the curriculum, because each teacher needs to know what he or she can expect when taking over a new class. This also implies that the principal and/or experienced senior teachers check that the whole teaching staff is following the jointly agreed upon program and academic targets. Experienced teachers are also better than beginners at developing the proper disciplined classroom atmosphere. In effective schools, where a collegial spirit prevails, they can give valuable advice. A healthy school spirit helps to reduce staff burnout and staff turnover, which in turn eases the maintenance of collegiality and continuity. This helps good teaching. In particular, scheduling teachers to stay with the same class of students over several years has several advantages. It permits teachers to get better acquainted with their students and to adjust their teaching methods to the students' individual needs. Also, such a policy promotes teachers' accountability, because it is less possible to blame the shortcomings of the class on the previous teacher.

The importance of the principal cannot be overrated. Ultimately it is he or she who sets the aims of the school, sets the tone and directs the effort. The good principal is highly visible and accessible to everybody: students, teachers and parents. Leadership is, ultimately, an art; it cannot be taught. But the principal of the effective school must have also an additional trait: he or she must like to teach. Often enough those teachers who dislike teaching try to escape it by becoming principals. They bury themselves in administrative details and never become leaders of truly effective schools.

The various aspects of effective schools are discussed in detail in an IRPP monograph by Peter Coleman.[6]

NOTES

1. Michael Rutter, B. Maughan, P. Mortimore, J. Ouston and A. Smith, *Fifteen Thousand Hours: Secondary Schools and their Effect on Children* (Cambridge, MA: Harvard University Press, 1979).
2. James S. Coleman and Thomas Hoffer, *Public and Private Schools: The Impact of Communities* (New York: Basic Books, 1987).
3. Michael Rutter, "School Effects on Pupil Progress," *Child Development*, Vol. 54, no. 1 (February 1983); and Stewart C. Purkey and Marshall S. Smith, "Effective Schools: A Review," *The Elementary School Journal*, Vol. 83, no. 1 (March 1983).
4. Archie E. Lapointe, Nancy A. Mead and Janice Askew, *Learning Mathematics* (Princeton, NJ: Educational Testing Service, 1992); and Archie E. Lapointe, Nancy A. Mead and Janice Askew, *Learning Science* (Princeton, NJ: Educational Testing Service, 1992).
5. L.W. Anderson, D.W. Ryan and B.J. Shapiro (eds.), *The IEA Classroom Environment Study* (Oxford: Pergamon Press, 1989).
6. Peter Coleman, *Learning About Schools: What Parents Need to Know and How They Can Find Out* (Montreal: Institute for Research on Public Policy, 1994).

EDUCATIONAL POLICY QUESTIONS

THE CURRICULUM

The international studies of student achievement distinguish between the intended curricula (what the educational authorities expected to be taught), the implemented curricula (what the teachers actually taught) and the attained curricula (what the pupils mastered). Students are unlikely to learn what is not in the implemented curriculum; and teachers are unlikely to teach what is not in the intended curriculum. What information do we have about the Canadian intended curriculum, as compared to that of other industrialized countries? The information is very fragmentary, but if we assume that the textbooks in use are an acceptable indication of the intended curriculum, we find that Alberta's educational authorities expect less from their students than the German, Japanese, Czech, or Hungarian authorities expect from theirs. The Mathematics and Science textbooks used in Alberta introduce topics several years later than in the comparison countries and treat the topics in less depth.[1] This is all the more disturbing because students in Alberta are among the best performing within Canada; the curricula of the other provinces are likely to be even less satisfying.

TEACHING STYLES

The traditional way of teaching (the teacher lectures, and corrects the exercises, the students listen, take notes and do exercises and homework) has proven its effectiveness over the centuries. Recent international studies indicate that it has not been superseded.[2] Table 10 shows that the traditional activities of lecturing, exercises and homework have a much stronger positive effect on student achievement than the recently fashionable policy of problem solving in groups and student-conducted experiments. This does not mean that research and reforms in pedagogy should be discounted or discouraged. It does mean that proposed reforms should be extensively tested on a large sample of students representative of the whole student body, under circumstances that will actually prevail after the reforms become general policy. Some proposed reforms may benefit a particular group of students while having a deleterious effect on others. Again, some reforms may require specially trained teachers, but it can be doubted that such teaching staff will be actually available. Peter Coleman gives an example of this in his IRPP monograph.[3]

STREAMING AND RELATED ISSUES

In 1984, the OECD Ministers of Education issued a declaration stating that "the goal of educating each child to the limits of her or his ability remains paramount..."[4] The mission statements of all the Canadian ministries of Education echo this sentiment, but practice does not accord with the professed intention. Already in the early grades, but certainly by the end of Grade 8, there is a difference in achievement equivalent to several grades between the strongest and weakest students. For example in the Second International Mathematical Study, a representative sample of about 4,000 Ontario students were given the same set of test problems at the beginning, and then again at the end of the school year. About 25 percent of the participants scored higher at the *beginning* of Grade 8 than did the average at the *end* of the year. In effect, these students would have been capable of operating at Grade 9 level or higher. Another group of some 33 percent of the participants scored lower by the *end* of the school year than did the average at the *beginning* of the year. This second group was, in effect, achieving at Grade 7 level or lower.

Table 10

Effect of Teaching Styles on Student Achievement in 14 Industrialized Countries

Activity	Positive effect	Negative effect
Mathematics		
Amount of listening to Math lessons	8	2
Amount of doing Math exercises on own	9	0
Amount of problem solving in groups	2	11
Amount of Math testing	5	5
Amount of time spent on Math homework	9	0
Amount of time spent on all homework	9	1
Science		
Amount of listening to Science lessons	7	0
Amount of student conducted experiments	1	7
Amount of Science testing	3	3
Amount of time spent on Science homework	5	3
Amount of time spent on all homework	7	1

SOURCE: Archie E. Lapointe, Nancy A. Mead and Janice Askew, *Learning Mathematics* (Princeton, NJ: Educational Testing Service, 1992); and Archie E. Lapointe, Nancy A. Mead and Janice Askew, *Learning Science* (Princeton, NJ: Educational Testing Service, 1992).

Consider the problem of the Grade 9 teacher who has to teach a representative sample class of Ontario Grade 8 graduates. If he or she directs the level and speed of instruction at the weak students, then the strong ones will learn less than they should. This is a net loss for the bright kids; what is perhaps even worse, they may get so bored and "turned off" that they become discipline problems and/or may drop out. If, on the other hand, the teacher targets the bright group, the weaker ones will fall even further behind, lose all motivation, and *they* will drop out. Is there any solution to this problem? If we could assess the true capacity of each child, we could group them into classes accordingly and then set the level and speed of instruction for each in an optimal manner. Indeed, we find that *every* school system sorts its students. For instance Germany sorts them at the age of 12 into schools which lead at the age of 15 to an academic type school or to a very high quality vocational apprenticeship supplemented by part-time compulsory formal schooling. Japan's senior high schools chose as their mandate the teaching of students of some pre-determined achievement level, and refuse students who do not fit in with this aim. Until recently, Ontario sorted students at Grade 9 into Advanced, General and Basic programs of differing difficulty.

Unfortunately, experience has shown that, at least in North America, we are not very good at sorting students correctly. The Second International Mathematical Study found severe mis-classifications in the United States. This has tragic consequences. Usually only the top stream has the curriculum and the "opportunity to learn" that qualify the student for university entrance. The mis-classification becomes a self-fulfilling prediction and has life-long consequences for the victim. In addition, being sorted into the General and Basic streams has motivation-destroying effects on many students. Almost all the Ontario drop-outs come from these streams. This is all the worse because we do not have the excellent German system, which permits the particularly able and ambitious vocational student eventually to rejoin the academic stream by progressing to university.

Is it possible to solve, or at least mitigate this problem? The Japanese primary schools, which, by the way, do not have the high-pressure, drill and memorization emphasis of their senior high schools, succeed without sorting to bring practically all pupils to the same, and by Canadian standards very high, level. How is this achieved? I have already alluded to the differences in the attitude of the pupils and their families.

In addition, the Japanese teacher has a very different working day compared to his or her North American counterpart. The length of the working day is similar, but the Japanese teacher spends at most 60 percent of the working time on classroom teaching. The rest is devoted to the preparation of lectures, correction of homework and of seatwork and to direct one-on-one contact with pupils. The tradeoff is in the class size. On the average, Japanese classes have 42 pupils, while Canadians have usually fewer than 30. In Japan, experienced and successful teachers are given one-year leaves to observe and mentor young and inexperienced colleagues. Differences in the achievement of Japanese students begin to show up during the junior high school years, and become very big in the last three years of secondary schooling.

If destreaming without deleterious consequences can be achieved at all, it can be done only by exerting the necessary effort needed to keep differences in educational achievement among the students to the unavoidable minimum *from Grade 1 on*. Unfortunately no such effort is being made in Ontario. In consequence it is unlikely that the present policy of destreaming Grade 9, to be followed soon by the same for Grade 10, will have a beneficial effect. On the contrary, it is likely to deteriorate the already mediocre record of the province even further. It will result either in lower achievement of the strong students or in a higher drop-out rate of the weak ones.

1. Alberta Chamber of Resources, *International Comparisons in Education: Curriculum, Values and Lessons* (Edmonton: Alberta Education, 1992).

2. Archie E. Lapointe, Nancy A. Mead and Janice Askew, *Learning Mathematics* (Princeton, NJ: Educational Testing Service, 1992); and Archie E. Lapointe, Nancy A. Mead and Janice Askew, *Learning Science* (Princeton, NJ: Educational Testing Service, 1992).

3. Peter Coleman, *Learning About Schools: What Parents Need to Know and How They Can Find Out* (Montreal: Institute for Research on Public Policy, 1994).

4. "OECD Ministers Discuss Education in Modern Society" (Paris: OECD, 1985), document on general distribution, p. 45, as quoted in *School and Quality: An International Report* (Paris: OECD, 1989), p. 33.

CHAPTER TEN

SCHOOL CHOICE

Why are schools with strong ethos relatively rare? Children differ in abilities, interests, motivation, career ambitions. One method of teaching, appropriate to some pupils, may not be the optimal one with others. The same applies to the curriculum, to methods for achieving discipline and to generating motivation. Successful teaching and managing of schools have an element of art that cannot be reduced to uniformity and rules. However, the monopolistic nature of the public education system encourages bureaucratic management. Its rules will be shaped in such a manner as to cause the minimum dissatisfaction of the public — i.e., will tend toward a very low common denominator.

There are more and more calls for introducing some competition into the educational system by permitting the parents to choose the school for their children. Studies in the United States show that private and Catholic schools are achieving better scholastic results and have fewer discipline problems than the public schools, even after adjustment for the intellectual and socio-economic characteristics of the school intake. Furthermore, they achieve this at a lower cost per student. Advocates of school choice maintain that bureaucratic regulations should be reduced to a minimum and the schools should be permitted to define and strive to realize their mandate as they wish. Parents would choose the school of their preference, with the money following the students, perhaps through the use of vouchers. Proper variation in the amount covered by the voucher could make the necessary allowance according to the special needs of the child and according to the ability and willingness of the district to raise taxes for purposes of education.

Parental choice would show which schools do not meet the expectations and would force these institutions to shape up (perhaps with some short-term help from the school boards) or disappear. Such a system would have to permit the expansion of successful schools and the founding of new ones as long as they meet the (rather loosely defined) criteria of graduation, teacher certification and health and safety regulations set by the government authorities. Advocates of choice maintain that it would be beneficial for the whole student body. Currently the well-to-do can exercise choice by buying or renting accommodation in areas known for their good schools; choice would extend this advantage to all children.

Opponents of school choice raise a number of objections. Even if choice would have the long-term advantages its partisans claim, there would be serious short-term difficulties. Able students would quickly cluster into schools of already high reputation, leaving the weaker students in the schools of lower quality. But the literature of effective schools emphasizes that the creation of academic ethos requires a core of at least average ability students. Thus choice would make the development of a larger number of effective schools even more difficult than at present, and create even more inequality than we are experiencing now. Also, is it likely that the educational bureaucracy would permit the weak schools to close down and thereby admit the failure of the existing educational policy? Furthermore, an intelligent choice among schools by parents would be possible only if reliable indicators of quality were published on a regular and up-to-date basis. Can we obtain consensus on what these indicators should be and can they be collected and disseminated without an onerous and expensive bureaucratic effort? Note that test results as such are not an adequate measure of the quality of instruction: only the gain in knowledge, the value added, is a fair indicator. Also, it is an open question whether such information would be used by the parents at all, even if it were available.

The example of the Netherlands throws interesting light on these questions. In that country, school choice has been available for about 90 years, and roughly two-thirds of all schools are private. The Dutch Constitution declares that all people are free to provide education; all private primary schools that satisfy the conditions laid down by Act of Parliament shall be financed from public funds according to the same standards as public-authority schools; and all schools can choose their own curricula. The government sets the final exams for the secondary schools. Even though the principals and teachers have considerable freedom to shape the contents and methods of instruction, there is little difference among the schools. Parents make their choice based on religious preferences, socio-economic characteristics of the existing student body, and/or the convenient location of the school rather than on the curriculum or the effectiveness of the teaching methods.[1] Schools regard it as unprofessional to publicize their students' achievement in their advertisements. Government regulation of schools has increased in the last decades because there is growing social consensus that the public has to be protected from incompetent schools.

What, then, can we expect from school choice? It would, to some degree, force schools to become more accountable to the public, and this would be a good thing. Those parents who care about their children's education would have an additional guide to choose. But not all parents care, and among those who do not all are qualified to make the right judgment. We do not choose our medical treatment on the basis of market decisions only. Lay people may feel the symptoms but do not have the professional expertise to choose the right treatment. Also, due to the cumulative nature of education, the effect of the treatment shows up with a considerable delay, namely during the whole subsequent life of the student.

1. Karen Seashore Louis and Boudewijn A. M. van Velzen, "School Choice in the Netherlands," *The Education Digest*, Vol. 56, no. 6 (February 1991), pp. 12-16.

SUMMARY: EDUCATION AND SOCIETY

Canada compares favourably with most industrialized countries in terms of years of schooling and of the percentage of gross domestic product spent on education. Unfortunately, these indicators throw light only on the *quantity* of education, not on its *quality*. The available data suggest that the high school system does not prepare our young people adequately for a working life. Serious vocational training begins only at the community college level or in apprenticeship; therefore it takes more time and public resources than in other countries. Another weakness of our system is that the students aiming at a university education are receiving a less intensive curriculum than those in the countries that lead in the international studies.

The strengths and weaknesses of our educational system are the reflections of various characteristics of Canadian society. The egalitarian streak in Canada's social attitudes manifests itself in the accessibility of primary and secondary education. As for the weaknesses, they, too, reflect aspects of society. Canada was one of those few victorious nations that emerged from the Second World War without damage to industrial capacity. In addition, Canada was politically stable and rich in natural resources. These advantages provided us with a high and improving standard of living for three decades and led to a dangerous level of complacency. We ascribed our comfortable life to the superiority of our institutions and were blind to the progress made by others. In the language of the economist we became a "satisficing" society rather than a "maximizing" one. We tended to rest on our laurels if things were "good enough," and we thought the prevailing educational system *was* "good enough." As in the field of international comparative productivity, so in the field of education the awakening is coming slowly and painfully.

Today our academic stream is doing poorer than the best foreign ones. Much of the post-secondary education is devoted to making up for what the secondary education system did not teach at an earlier age and at a lower cost, though it should have done so. Thomas Rohlen estimates that "...the average Japanese high school graduate has the equivalent basic knowledge of the average American college graduate."[1] Even though the cognitive achievement of the Canadian students is higher than that of the Americans, we do worse than the best performers in the international studies. This was not known until the early 1980s and the knowledge is very slow to sink in. Indeed, while a small vocal minority is expressing concern, it is far from being regarded as a major and pressing problem by the public at large. There is no sense of a national emergency.

Having observed the disadvantages under which suffer those who have not finished high school, Canadian society has reacted with curriculum dilution and/or grade inflation. For instance, according to the Ministry of Education, Ontario, in 1965/66, 3.0 percent of Ontario high school graduates received a grade average of 80 percent, that is qualified as Ontario Scholars.[2] By 1991/92 the percentage increased to 18.2.[3] The consequence is a massive devaluation of the graduation diploma. It is no longer a guarantee even of functional literacy and numeracy, a modest enough requirement.

Vocational education is in a very poor shape. This is both the effect and cause of the low prestige of craftsmanship in Canada. Parents are trying their best to keep their children in the streams that lead to post-secondary education; in consequence, there is little inducement for educational policy makers to upgrade the quality and equipment of vocational courses in the public system. In the countries with the best vocational training, either the employers provide the training (Japan) or there is a joint (dual) system of co-operation between employers and the public system (Germany). In Canada, employers are not much interested in investing in employee training because they fear that well-trained workers will be hired away by competitors, and the firm doing the training will not recoup its investment, even less gain a return on it. If this fear is justified then there is a clear divergence between social and private interest, a case of what the economists call "market failure," and society is justified in intervening by providing the needed education or training. The question remains whether the public would be willing to provide the needed expenditure for a branch of schooling that has not proven it can provide high-quality graduates with promising employment prospects. Here, once again, we are confronted by a vicious circle.

Our biggest educational problems are the consequences of societal attitudes. This fact, plus the numerous vicious circles mentioned in this monograph, are the reasons why it is so difficult to make *real* changes (rather than pretended ones) in educational policy. It is well known that in the field of education things change with glacial slowness in most countries. Yet there is proof that rapid change is possible, if there is a will. In the late 1950s, less than half of Japanese youngsters graduated from high school. By 1980, some 90 percent did so. This was a stupendous change in less than a generation. Canada's traditional comparative advantages having been eroded, we must develop new ones. An outstanding educational system is not a sufficient condition of future high productivity and prosperity, but it is a necessary one.

1. Thomas P. Rohlen, *Japan's High Schools* (Berkeley, CA: University of California Press, 1983).
2. Ministry of Education, Ontario, fax from Tim Fisher, January 10, 1994.
3. See also Gilbert Plaw, "Quebec Education Ministry Promotes Grade Inflation," *The Gazette*, May 26, 1994, p. B3; Council of Deans of Engineering, *Submission to Ontario's Royal Commission on Learning*, mimeo, 1993; and Dennis Raphael, "From Bad to Worse: Student Achievement in Ontario," *The Globe and Mail*, April 27, 1993, p. A23.

CHAPTER TWELVE

A RESEARCH PROPOSAL

This monograph touched on a number of factors that influence educational achievement. Some operate on the level of the individual student, some are characteristics of his or her family, peers, teachers, schools, school boards and of the educational policy of their respective provinces. These factors have *direct* effects on the achievement of the student, but may also *interact* with each other. For instance, a particular teaching technique may be highly successful with mediocre students, but may be "off-putting" for particularly bright ones.[1] Another example: some immigrant children may be performing better than average in science or mathematics, but poorer in reading and writing.

Due to the cumulative nature of education, these influences on the achievement of individuals show up gradually during the school years, and then reveal their effect on the productivity, earning power, success and happiness over the rest of the individual's life. In order to be able to conduct an intelligent educational policy, it would be necessary to quantify both the direct *and* interactive effects. Unfortunately, this information is not available. It would be very important and useful to generate it. How could this be done? By a large-scale study as sketched out below.

The suggested procedure is represented in diagram 1. The student can be described at time zero (say, the beginning of Grade 1) by certain personal characteristics like motivation, cognitive achievement, health status and so on. The student is also strongly influenced by his or her home characteristics (for instance the parents' or guardians' expectations, socio-economic status, the number of siblings). This is represented in Diagram 1 by the solid arrow pointing from the home to the student. To a lesser extent (reflected in diagram 1 by the dashed arrow) the student may influence the home as well (for instance his or her physical or mental problems may increase the stress in the home, leading to a marital breakdown). During the school year, the personal and family characteristics interact with school-based influences: those of the teachers, of the school as an organization and the student's peers.

The teachers can be characterized in a variety of ways, for instance by their number, experience, qualifications (all of which are reflected also in the amount of dollars devoted to remunerating their services) and by their educational processes and classroom practices. Similarly, the school as an organization may act on the student both through its resources (labs, computers, sport facilities), which can be described in physical terms or in dollars, and through its educational and disciplinary processes and school ethos. The effect of peers on the individual student is a generally acknowledged fact, while the individual may have a reciprocal, though probably minor, effect on his or her peers.

The school ethos influences teacher characteristics and — to a lesser extent — the latter feed back on the school characteristics. The spirit of the school is expected to have a major effect on the student body (the individual student's peers), and this influence is reciprocal. The characteristics of the school are influenced by the directives of its school board, which is in turn subject to the policies of its provincial department of Education.

The interactions of all these influences during the school year result in the outcomes of Year 1 (gain in knowledge and skills, work discipline, socialization and so on), which feed back on the student's characteristics and become the starting conditions for Year 2. Thus every round's initial conditions, inputs and outcomes influence the outcomes of the subsequent rounds. There may also be other new, exogenous forces or events acting on the student (e.g., illness).

School outcomes may influence the home as well. In some instances, good or bad educational outcomes may raise or lower the family's educational expectations for the child. In other cases, a poor outcome may spur

Diagram 1

Hypothetical Model of the Educational Process

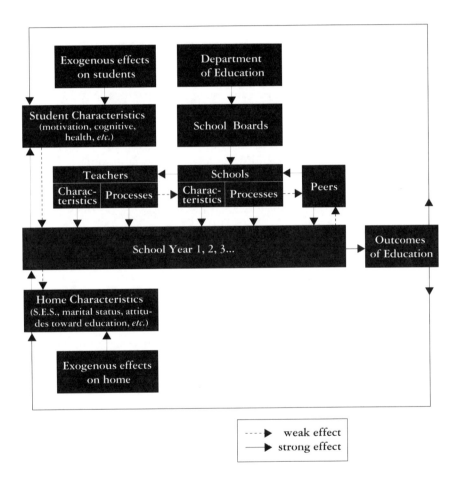

the family to greater efforts to remediate the situation. In addition to the educational outcomes of Year 1, the home may be also subject to relevant new exogenous influences (e.g., job loss, bereavement) which may influence the student's performance in Year 2.

In order to realize a research program by which to explore the interactions of all these factors, it would be necessary to survey a very substantial cohort of six year-olds (say 10,000 to 15,000 individuals) and then follow and re-survey them individually over a long period. The survey findings would start to yield valuable results practically from the very beginning (e.g., the effect of home *versus* school influences in the acquisition of basic skills; the dispersion of student achievement under various teaching styles), but its value would grow tremendously with the increasing length of the project, particularly if it continues tracking the individuals up to the age of, say, 40. This is the age at which a similar Swedish study found the full effect of education on earning power.[2]

A project of this size would need very substantial resources, both in terms of money and highly qualified manpower. Today, probably only Statistics Canada would be able to provide the needed capacity in survey and sample design and analytic evaluation necessary to do the job properly; even that institution would need substantial additional financing. It would be highly desirable that the provinces put aside their traditional hostility toward federal research in the field of education and actively participate in such a project. Canada is the only federation whose central government does no work in educational research. We cannot afford to continue such petty jurisdictional jealousy.

If cost and resource limitations make such a long research horizon too intimidating, then I would urge *very emphatically* that the project should zero in on the first eight years of schooling. Both the equity and the efficiency aspects of education require that we learn how to combine a higher level of cognitive achievement with a reduced level of its dispersion.

Canadian society would derive benefits vastly greater than the significant outlay and resources required for such a project.

N o t e s

1. R.E. Snow, "Aptitude — Treatment Interaction Models of Teaching," in Husen and Postlethwaite (eds.), *The International Encyclopedia of Education,* (Oxford, New York: Pergamon Press, 1985).
2. Albert Tuijnman, *Recurrent Education, Earnings and Well-Being: A Fifty-Year Longitudinal Study of A Cohort of Swedish Men* (Stockholm: Almquist and Wicksell International, 1989).

RESPONSES

BY

ROBERT K. CROCKER

AND

GERALDINE GILLISS

———

R O B E R T   K .   C R O C K E R

T H O M A S   S C H W E I T Z E R ' S   R E P O R T   C A R D   O N   T H E

S T A T E   O F   E D U C A T I O N   I N   C A N A D A :

A   C O M M E N T A R Y   O N   M A K I N G   T H E   G R A D E

The education system of this country is, in many important respects, a product of the 1960s. Although the basic structures of schooling have been in place since the late 19th century, developments such as child-centred teaching, services to children with special needs or disabilities, broad curriculum, social promotion, curriculum differentiation and a host of other changes to the ways in which teaching and learning take place are all products of an educational transformation which can be traced to social reforms of 30 years ago, coupled with a major curriculum reform movement of the same era.

Throughout the 1970s and 1980s, education experienced a low public profile in most parts of Canada. Operation of the education system was left largely to the legion of professionals — teachers, principals, school board officials and provincial government bureaucrats, put in place during the 1960s to oversee the rapid expansion of programs and services at the time. The level of public satisfaction with education was relatively high (despite the conclusion reached by Thomas Schweitzer), and there were substantial improvements in participation rates and services to students who, in an earlier era, would never have been in regular schools.

Since the late 1980s, however, education has returned to the political agenda with substantial force. It is not difficult to identify the driving issues behind the current educational reform movement. A decade ago, we were unaware that Canada's performance by world standards was not as high as might be expected, given the substantial levels of investment in education in this country. A decade ago, the fiscal crisis that now affects all levels of government was just beginning to emerge. More important than either of these developments, however, are the effects of global economic change, the growth of information technology, the corresponding decline of traditional resource and manufacturing industries, the increased impact of technology on society and finally the emergence of educational reform movements in other countries, most notably the United States. All of these developments place a greater premium than ever before on higher levels of educational performance. It is fair to characterize the reforms of the 1960s as being driven by the desire to increase participation. On the other hand, the reforms of the 1990s are clearly driven by the demand for improved performance and greater accountability.

Schweitzer's monograph is a timely and useful contribution to the continuing debate over the quality of education in Canada. The essay helps bring to greater public attention the results of international and interprovincial comparative achievement testing. It also brings to the fore several profoundly important issues, such as streaming, quality of teaching and choice of schools, that have received far too little public attention. Unfortunately, Schweitzer attempts to cover far too much ground, and thus fails to explore these areas in the depth they deserve. The section on interprovincial and international test scores is the strongest, perhaps because it reflects the author's previous work. What is even more interesting and valuable is the discussion on the strengths and weaknesses of testing. Because testing has been controversial, most of the debate in this area has been carried out by advocates on both sides of the argument, and has shed more heat than light on the merits of testing.

This commentary follows the main sections of the monograph, in order to avoid introducing new issues into an already complex debate, and to ensure that Schweitzer's points are not lost in what could easily be a new essay on the policy issues raised. The perspective taken is that of one whose research activities have ranged from international achievement testing to comparative studies of the effectiveness of teaching, and who recently has had to make the transition from research to policy formulation.

THE PURPOSES OF EDUCATION

Attempting to set out any list of the purposes of education is a risky business. The truth is that the public expects a great deal from schools, and the list of possible educational goals is ever increasing. At the same time, simply giving a list, without reference to sources, or recourse to empirical evidence, at best appears arbitrary, and seems to represent one person's opinion. There is little to lead us to believe that there would be general agreement on the list of purposes given, as Schweitzer asserts.

A different approach could have been taken, which would have been much more relevant to the subsequent discussion. It would have been quite revealing to have drawn some inferences about the purposes of education from the public opinion polls. While not all such surveys have focussed on this issue, there are good indications from some polls as to the priorities the public would assign to various educational goals. In any case, the identification of goals is one of the areas in which it is most legitimate to use public opinion polls, because the goals of education should be established by the public and not by the professionals hired to see that these goals are achieved.

Another fruitful approach would have been to examine statements of the aims of education produced by the various provinces. These are fairly readily available, and would have shed substantial light on the question of whether any form of national consensus exists, or on whether there is any link between performance variations and differences in aims. Provincial governments have recently been busy restating their goals, typically in the form of now-fashionable "mission statements." For example, British Columbia has expressed the mandate of its school system very succinctly:

In a QUALITY EDUCATION system, schools have a primary responsibility for:
the intellectual development of students and a shared responsibility for the human and social development, and career development of students. As well, schools should exhibit the following attributes:

Accessibility
Relevance
Equity
Quality
Accountability[1]

The Government of Newfoundland has also recently stated a specific goal for the reform of education.

The goal is to transform the system from one of persistent under-performance to one in which achievement levels rank with the best in the nation.[2]

These statements clearly place intellectual development at the forefront of educational goals. Most recent policy statements from other provinces convey a similar tone.

This brings me to the most important point. In Schweitzer's monograph, there is virtually no link between the statements of purposes and any of the subsequent discussion. At the same time, the major sections on access and achievement speak directly to the goals presented in the above statements. While the attention to achievement is certainly not misplaced, when the above goals are considered, it is not clear that the objectives outlined in the paper are as readily identified with achievement. For example, working backward from the section on achievement, one would infer that an important goal should be something like "Canadian students should be expected to score as high as or higher than those in other countries on standardized tests of mathematics and science." Similarly, it might be inferred from the section on accessibility that keeping students in school as long as possible should be the goal. These goals are much more specific, and much more in tune with the provincial statements, than some of the ones identified in the paper.

One of the major problems in education is, in fact, the gap between goal statements and what schools can reasonably be expected to accomplish. For example, while it is difficult to argue with the goal of good citizenship, schooling is only one means, and not necessarily the most important means, of achieving this goal. The problem here is more with the goals than with the accomplishments. By stating goals that are much too global and diffuse, we are setting schools up for failure, both because the goals themselves cannot be measured, and because they set out impossible expectations for schools. It is much more reasonable to state attainable goals, especially those toward which the school can be expected to make a unique contribution, and which could not be achieved by any other means. High academic achievement is an example of such a realistic goal.

ACCESSIBILITY

Interestingly enough, accessibility is a goal of education that we seem to take for granted. Universal access is so widely accepted that it is hardly an issue. Nevertheless, we should keep two things in mind. The first is that access is not an end in itself, is no guarantee of participation and is certainly no assurance of achievement. In fact, as Schweitzer points out, access in Canada is universal up to the end of secondary education. What varies is the choices exercised by students, once they reach legal school-leaving age. Some stay and some leave. Some perform at high levels, and some at very low levels.

The second point is that access is a moving target. At one time, universal access to elementary education was the goal. Obviously we no longer hear of students not completing elementary school. However, the fact that we hear a great deal about drop-outs from secondary school indicates that universal access to the end of secondary education is the current target, and that it has not quite been reached. In view of increasing demand in the workforce, universal access to some form of post-secondary education can be expected to be the next goal, even though current financial constraints make it difficult to see how this can be accomplished.

The comparative data on years of schooling, presented in Schweitzer's Table 2, is problematic because it confuses the issue of access with that of participation. The relatively low participation rate in the United Kingdom, for example, can be accounted for by the fact that universal access ends when students reach age 16. Despite relatively low participation, as indicated by the comparative data, the drop-out rate in Britain is essentially zero, because universal schooling ends just at the legal school-leaving age, and because almost all students exit with some form of general certificate. More advanced studies, comparable to (but more rigorous than) our last years of high school, are accessible only to a small number of students. Bringing this into a Canadian context, it can be argued that the drop-out problem in Canada can be solved simply by aligning the legal school-leaving age with the age needed to attain the final year of secondary schooling.

The relationship of years of schooling to the job market is equally problematic. This is where a more comprehensive analysis of the economic impact of education is badly needed. While it is clear from the data that both employment levels and income are related to educational levels, what is not clear is whether this relationship is causal. It is entirely possible, for example, that a universal increase or decrease in educational levels may have no impact on overall employment. The system might simply adjust to the new reality. To illustrate the point, high school graduates may enjoy higher employment rates than high school drop-outs simply because, in a competitive job market, a diploma may merely be used as a convenient screening device, not because the skills acquired by high school graduates are needed in the job market, or because those with a diploma will perform better than those without. Going a step further, while a high school diploma may make an individual more competitive, it may do nothing to increase the number of jobs available. If the job market is a zero sum game, there is no particular value to the system as a whole in increasing the participation rate.

Conventional wisdom, of course, is that the job market is not a zero sum game, and that higher levels of education in the population as a whole can have a positive overall economic impact. The simplest case of this would be a situation of shortages of personnel in areas demanding high levels of education and shortages of jobs at the opposite extreme. Increasing educational levels would then create a greater match between available jobs and available people to fill these jobs. A more general scenario would be that more highly educated people are better able to create economic activity — by being more entrepreneurial for example. Finally, economic advantage for a particular nation might be created in a global market, if that nation has available a supply of workers in high demand areas where there is a global shortage of workers. Economic activity might thus shift toward such countries in order to take advantage of a highly educated work force. (This phenomenon would be the opposite of economic activity moving to areas of low labour costs.)

I am not attempting to argue that any of these scenarios is the correct one. The point is that any serious economic analysis of educational benefits ought to investigate such hypotheses. Unfortunately, economists seem not to have turned their attention seriously to this matter, and we continue to rely on conventional wisdom, supported by correlational data, about the relationship of education to jobs.

PUBLIC OPINION

The value of using public opinion as an indicator of educational quality also raises problems. While it seems straightforward to argue that public satisfaction with our education system is desirable, it is by no means obvious that there is a positive relationship between public satisfaction and actual performance. In fact, some of the polls cited by Schweitzer suggest an inverse relationship when interprovincial comparisons are examined. In other words, there is some indication in the poll data that the lowest performing provinces tend to have the highest levels of satisfaction. Although this issue has not been pursued in detail, the possibility of a "complacency" hypothesis should not be overlooked: it is again possible to reverse the assumed direction of causality, and argue that low performance may be a result of public contentment with the levels we have been achieving. Certainly a system in which there is no particular press to improve is at risk of being or becoming mediocre.

Rather than looking at public satisfaction as an indicator of quality, it is more reasonable to use public opinion surveys as a tool for examining goals and priorities, gauging public willingness to pay for education, establishing general curriculum priorities and for similar purposes. For example, Schweitzer's analysis of goals would have been much more persuasive had this been backed by public views on their relative importance. Similarly, much more could be learned from a public expression of willingness to pay the necessary taxes than from a public "grading" of the system. Taking the point a step further, it is not obvious whether public dissatisfaction should be used as an argument for increased or reduced funding. Some would use public dissatisfaction with educational productivity as evidence that the system is underfunded. Others could reverse this argument, and hold that an under-productive system is, by definition, overfunded for the results produced.

In any case, contrary to Schweitzer's conclusion, I would read the levels of satisfaction expressed in the various polls to be quite high. Studies comparing education to other enterprises (including some of those cited in the monograph) have generally borne this out. Schweitzer arrives at his conclusions about dissatisfaction by the curious device of adding several of the lower categories together and then comparing the result to the number of A grades. Similarly, he argues that the public is less satisfied with performance in language than in science and mathematics, although the results show only fairly small differences, particularly in the number indicating dissatisfaction. He then goes on to draw the conclusion that this may be due to the lower levels of education of an earlier generation, whose members may be less able to judge performance in mathematics and science. Aside from the possibility that there are other explanations for this observation, a simple age breakdown of the respondents would have shed some light on the conclusion at hand.

OBJECTIVE MEASURES

By objective measures, Schweitzer refers particularly to a number of national and international testing programs conducted over the past decade or so. This section is the strongest part of the monograph. At the same time, it is not clear whether the major emphasis is on the actual levels of achievement or on the observed differences between countries or provinces. The questions that should have been asked are "how good are Canadian schools at producing outcomes in core subject areas, what are the differences between provinces and how might these results be accounted for?" This would have permitted a more elaborated analysis of an area that the author has investigated in depth, and that deserves to be better known. The relatively cursory treatment of these data raises as many questions as are answered, and leaves the impression that the author is more interested in supporting a predetermined conclusion of poor performance than in asking what the data really tell us.

The problem begins with the choice of three different methods of presenting the data. The summary given in Table 2 uses rankings, and the IAEP results presented in Charts 1 and 2 use difference scores. The difference in score approach is continued in the interprovincial comparisons on the SAIP mathematics test, but the units switch to differences in "levels" in which a five-point scale has been used. The approach taken by SAIP is fairly complex, and it is difficult to make much of the results without a more detailed explanation of the scale used. A presentation parallel to that used by SAIP itself, in which the proportion of students at each level formed the basis for comparison, would have been more help-ful. As it stands, the average reader would be left with the impression that the differences between provinces are quite small numerically, but quite large proportionally (because of the large scale used in the chart), neither of which is a reasonable conclusion. In fact, most of the inter-provincial differences in SAIP mathematics were not statistically signifi-cant, and were certainly too small to be of practical significance. The only question therefore is whether these levels of performance are satisfactory.

Finally it must be noted that there is nothing in the data to justify some of the conclusions reached. For example, the statement that "Canadian students tended to do relatively better in the 1980s than in the 1990s" is not at all supported by Table 7. In fact, a comparison of the relative rankings for all of the studies in the two decades reveals an almost identical pattern, with Canada high in some rankings and low in others. In any case, the number of comparisons available is insufficient to draw any conclusion. This is an important point, because it is used to support the inference, which recurs throughout the monograph, that Canada's performance is deteriorating.

The latter inference is strongest in the brief section devoted to the Canadian Test of Basic Skills. Unfortunately, the report cited as the basis for the conclusion is not readily available. It can only be assumed that the report is based on the samples used in the periodic recalibrations of the test. If the results indeed show a deterioration of performance, then this is a very serious matter. This is the most obvious example of where a more elaborated presentation is required. The nature of the longitudinal study, and the actual results, need to be presented before the validity of the conclusion can be assessed. Large-scale use has been made of the CTBS in various jurisdictions. Data from such administrations would shed substantial light on changes over time.

The section on the value of tests as measures of the quality of educa-tion is a useful contribution. While this issue is hotly debated among proponents and opponents of testing, it is rare to find an attempt to explain the possible interpretations of tests, especially in a document designed for a public audience. Greater public understanding of norma-tive *versus* criterion-referenced test interpretations is crucial to our ability to advance the debate over the use of tests. Such understanding might reduce the prevalence of headlines such as *"Students Shine in Language Tests"* which recently appeared in a local newspaper. In reality, the test results showed that Newfoundland students were on a par with those elsewhere in Canada on the 1994 SAIP Writing Assessment, but told us nothing about the actual levels of performance, or whether such performance was satisfactory or unsatisfactory by some standard.

PROBLEM AREAS

If the section on test results is the strongest of the monograph, the discussion of students, family and teaching is the weakest. Without wishing to argue that these issues can be understood only be educators, it must be said that it is impossible to do justice to such complex topics within the limits of a short popular monograph.

The section on students shows a promising beginning, in identifying effort and motivation as primary contributors to achievement. However, like other important issues, these are given relatively cursory treatment. The discussion on the effects of part-time work is even distracting, since no real evidence exists on the impact on school achievement of work relative to other activities such as watching television. Work is confined almost entirely to high school students and cannot be used to account for the poor performance of elementary school students. No data are presented on how many students actually work, or on the average or range of work hours. While common sense suggests that work weeks of 20 hours or more would be detrimental, only an extremely small proportion of students work such hours, and many of these have made a deliberate decision to be part-time students, for various reasons. In any case, many studies indicate that, on average, television viewing is the most prevalent out-of-school activity, and affects students at all levels. It would certainly be more useful to focus on television viewing than on work as a distraction from school achievement.

The discussion of work, along with the reference to remediation, serves to remind us that one of the primary variables in achievement is time. A much more complete analysis could have been presented had the initial question been one of how time is used and how it might best be used. As a set of alternative propositions, the following might be offered:

1. Time is the single most important resource at our disposal.

2. The current organization of the school is based on a fixed-time model.

3. A more sensible organization would incorporate variable times

for different students, in order to attain higher levels of achievement more uniformly .

4.   Remediation is only one way of saying that we wish to give more time to some students than to others.

Essentially, what needs to be considered in organizing schooling is how to restructure the system to permit greater emphasis on time and effort, and in particular to find more time for those who need it most. A variety of arrangements are possible, from non-gradedness to greater emphasis on core subjects for those having difficulty, to longer school days or years. The latter could include summer sessions for those who need to catch up, as an alternative to grade repetition and other devices for keeping students behind. A strong argument can be made that time is the most valuable resource available to improve achievement. Time is also one of the easiest variables to manipulate through administrative arrangements. All that is required is a determination to use time to greatest advantage. Unfortunately, this requires a strong commitment on the part of students and teachers, as well as home and system support. It is by no means certain that Canadian society is ready to take additional time from other activities in pursuit of higher achievement.

Even more troublesome is the discussion of the use of resources, and in particular the reliance on the work of Erik Hanushek as the basis for the conclusion that resource inputs are of little consequence. We must grant, of course, that it is doubtful the high cost of education in Canada is justified by the results. Nevertheless, more sophisticated analyses than the simple box scores compiled by Hanushek reveal much more substantial relationships between inputs and achievement.[3] In any case, many of the conclusions presented are simply inconsistent with the results given. For example, Table 9 shows that administrative inputs give positive results in seven studies, and negative results in only one, with more than 50 studies showing no effect (the most plausible conclusion in this instance). Yet Schweitzer concludes that administrative inputs have a detrimental effect on achievement. Similarly, the highly favourable box score for teaching experience is dismissed as "not overwhelming" despite the fact that the table gives no indication of the strength of any of the relationships.

The most serious difficulty is with the discussion of class size. First, it is not reasonable to conclude that decreasing class size by, say, one third would yield an increase of 50 to 100 percent in costs. Certain educational costs are fixed, and others are more closely related to use rather than availability of personnel. To take a simple example, it is possible to find classes as large as 35 in Newfoundland schools, despite the existence of a 15:1 pupil/teacher ratio. Significant reductions in class size could be achieved with no additional personnel if more teachers were deployed to classroom duties, rather than to other work. If we believe that smaller classes can have a positive effect on achievement, and there is good evidence to this effect, then there are ways to achieve this without a significant increase in resources.

More relevant is the observation that only small effects on achievement are found for classes in the normal range of 20 to 40. The counterpoint, also made in the Glass and Smith review cited, is that creating very small classes has highly salutary effects. One can argue that we need to organize schools so as to create small classes in the core subjects, where achievement is most important, at the expense of larger classes in more peripheral areas of the curriculum.

While there is a body of research[4] that clearly supports whole class teaching or direct instruction, work on such strategies as cooperative learning[5] calls the direct instruction approach into question. Such research indicates that alternative ways of organizing students within a class can have positive effects compared to regular whole class teaching. The most plausible explanation for these apparently conflicting results is that the teaching strategies typically used in contrast to direct instruction have tended to involve less emphasis on academic achievement, and greater emphasis on other outcomes. Cooperative learning, on the other hand, is clearly an achievement-oriented approach.

STREAMING

The persistence of various forms of streaming in schools, in the face of strong evidence of its detrimental effects on the very students it is designed to help — namely those at the lower end of the achievement spectrum — is a classic example of the triumph of political and organizational considerations over academic ones. This section of Schweitzer's paper hints at the major source of the problem with streaming, but unfortunately suggests that the move toward destreaming is destined to fail because we have not learned to cope with the variations in ability normally found in classrooms.

This is where a lesson can be learned form Japanese primary education, as Schweitzer hints, but does not fully develop. The problem lies in the fundamental assumption, which seems to be accepted without question in North American education, that the goal is to educate every child to the limits of his or her ability. This close coupling of educational prospects with ability is, in many aspects of education, also associated with another assumption, namely that children at the lower end of the ability spectrum cannot be expected to achieve well in school and hence should be sorted into streams where the curriculum is more closely matched to their ability. In contrast, Japanese primary education is organized on an undifferentiated cooperative model, in which it is assumed that everyone can achieve at high levels and, more important, that achievement is associated with effort rather than ability.[6] In Japan, low achievement is attributed to insufficient effort, whereas in North America, low achievement is more typically attributed to low ability.

In light of the Japanese experience, the premise that achievement is a function of ability should be replaced by the premise that achievement is a function of effort. A close correlation between ability and achievement must be acknowledged. However, it does not necessarily follow that low ability is the cause of low achievement. The relationship may be the reverse, or it may be an artifact of the similarity of the types of instruments used to measure both ability and achievement. In any case, even if the relationship is causal in the direction assumed, this relationship is not a particularly fruitful basis for organizing an education system, for the simple reason that it condemns low ability students to low achievement, rather than encouraging us to organize to attenuate or overcome any disadvantage of low ability.

Schweitzer makes a valuable point when he concludes that moving to destreaming, without solving the problem of wide ranges of achievement in a class, can be as detrimental as streaming. The potential solution to this dilemma lies in challenging the basic assumption that such wide ranges of achievement are inevitable, or are cumulative as students progress through the grades. Organizing schools to place greater emphasis on effort is one of the most important ways in which the range of achievement can be narrowed, and the overall level of achievement increased.

SCHOOL CHOICE

Much has been made of the issue of school choice in recent years. Advocacy for choice comes mainly from two sources. The first is essentially driven by an ideology, which places great store on competition as the driving force for improvement. The second is a source widely overlooked by mainstream educators — religion. Ongoing controversy in Ontario over Catholic education, and the right of other religious groups to similar treatment, along with the much more contentious issue in Newfoundland over the right of churches to control their own schools, illustrate this point. Religious schooling advocates, in particular, tend to base their argument on the United Nations Declaration of Human Rights, which states that "parents have the fundamental right to choose the type of education for their children." This line of argument would place choice as the first principle of education, and hence would require that education be organized with this in mind.

The competition agenda is different in the sense that choice is a device for injecting competition, and hence for improving outcomes, rather than a matter of human rights. Nevertheless, the implications for organizing the school system are essentially the same. Either ideology could be advanced by proponents of voucher systems, charter schools or other devices through which like-minded groups can establish their own schools, with equal access to public funds. Schweitzer rightly points out that choice is a two-edged sword, and that there are many drawbacks to building a system based on choice. The Netherlands example is a good one, because that country has usually performed reasonably well in international comparative studies.

What is overlooked in almost all arguments over choice is the simple matter of demographics. The ability to offer choice is almost entirely confined to densely populated urban areas, where it is feasible to establish more than one school in the same locality. In general, the greater the choice, the smaller the schools are likely to become. While there is some argument over whether economies of scale apply generally in education (there are no economies of scale if costs are directly proportional to enrolments), there is plenty of room for doubt whether very small schools can offer programs comparable to those available in mid-size to larger schools without making inordinate demands on resources. In rural areas, there is simply no way to organize a school system based on choice without creating very small schools, having long transportation distances, establishing residential schools or increasing the need for such services as distance education or home schooling, most of which result in added costs. One possibility would be to support all schools to the same level in public funds, and allow parents to pay any marginal costs associated with the exercise of choice. However, the movement toward choice does not appear anywhere near strong enough to justify the profound changes in school organization that would be required to implement such a system.

CONCLUDING OBSERVATIONS

This monograph conveys a highly pessimistic view of the state of education in Canada. While much of the data presented supports such a view, the tendency to over-interpret certain results, particularly the public opinion results and the achievement data, tends to weaken the case being made.

One can also read from the monograph a pessimistic outlook on the prospects for improvement. Unfortunately, the author has overlooked entirely the strong movement toward improvement that has emerged since about 1990. Whatever may be said about the limitations of the international achievement comparisons, these have provided substantial impetus to a trend toward a more focussed approach to education, with an emphasis on achievement. Such an approach had been absent from mainstream educational thinking for two decades. The results have reinforced an emerging grass-roots discontent, and a demand for greater accountability on the part of educators to the public.

The renewed emphasis on achievement is evident in virtually all studies of education over the past five years, and is clearly apparent in actions on the part of almost all of the provinces. From British Columbia to Newfoundland, and now finally in Ontario, major reports on education have pointed to the problems identified in this monograph, and have been surprisingly consistent in their recommendations for improvement. The most common threads underlying these reviews have been the need to develop higher standards, to ensure that students meet these standards, to develop measures of outcomes and to develop mechanisms for greater accountability. An undercurrent in most studies is the need to make more efficient use of the large-scale resources devoted to education. Nevertheless, despite the severe financial problems facing governments at all levels, it is clear that improved performance, rather than financial efficiency, is the main driving force for educational reform. Rarely a month goes by without a new policy document from some province or other about plans for educational reform, based on the need to improve performance. There is no doubt that political leaders are reacting to a grass-roots demand for improved performance.

Where is all of this activity likely to lead? The history of education is littered with failed efforts to reform. Nevertheless, the overall tendency has been in the direction of improved educational attainment and achievement. Each new movement brings with it some gain. For example, it is clear that the thrust of the past two decades has been toward increased participation. This thrust is most pronounced in the inclusion of students with disabilities into the educational mainstream, as well as in increased secondary and post-secondary participation rates. Even though, as Schweitzer argues, this gain may have been at the expense of achievement levels, we now have established a base upon which higher achievement can be built. Now that most students remain in school at least to the end of secondary education, the time is ripe to increase expectations and standards. It is unlikely that attempts to increase achievement will lead to a major increase in the number of drop-outs.

Finally, it appears that the time is ripe for a change from the basic premise that the goal of education is to educate children to the limits of their ability to the premise that the goal of education is to educate children to an established standard of achievement. While it may be argued that the latter goal is unattainable, an equally strong argument can be made that the former goal has also never been attained, because of the accompanying assumption that students who are below average in ability cannot be expected to achieve at high levels. More important, the limits of ability premise is essentially a pessimistic one, despite its intuitive appeal on a human rights level. The new premise is one which requires continued striving for improvement, rather than a complacent view that little can change because of limitations of ability. Acceptance of the view that achievement is a function of effort rather than ability can be expected to go further toward improving educational achievement than any other action we can take. The question is whether we have the ingenuity and the will to organize the education system in a manner consistent with this premise.

Notes

otes

Notes

1. British Columbia Ministry of Education, *Mandate of the Schools*, Victoria, BC, 1989.
2. Government of Newfoundland and Labrador, *Adjusting the Course-Part II: Improving the Conditions of Learning*, St. John's, 1994.
3. L.V. Hedges, R.D. Laine and R. Greenwald, "Does Money Matter?: A Meta-analysis of the Effects of Differential School Inputs on Student Outcomes," *Educational Researcher*, Vol. 23, no. 3 (April 1994), pp. 5-14.
4. B. Rosenshine, "Explicit Teaching," in D.C. Berliner and B. Rosenshine (eds.), *Talks to Teachers* (New York: Random House, 1987), pp. 75-92.
5. R.E. Slavin, "When Does Cooperative Education Increase Student Achievement?", *Psychological Bulletin*, Vol. 94 (1983), pp. 429-45.
6. S.D. Holloway, "Concepts of Ability and Effort in Japan and the United States," *Review of Educational Research*, Vol. 58, no. 3 (Fall 1988), pp. 327-45.

GERALDINE GILLISS

THE GRADE IS MADE IF ONE LOOKS

AT THE DATA CAREFULLY

I commend Thomas Schweitzer on certain aspects of his monograph. In particular, I liked his comments on the thorny subject of school choice. Although there are those who claim that a free market in schools would lead to better schools at lower cost, I am inclined, with Schweitzer, to believe that free choice would simply let more able students cluster in those schools which already enjoy higher reputations, to the detriment not only of our notion of equality, but to the educational chances of those left behind in schools of lower quality. Schweitzer should also be commended for his frequent references to the primary role of the parents in promoting the educational chances of their children.

Where I want to take issue is with his oft-repeated conclusion that Canadian education produces only mediocre results and that it is particularly weak at the Grade 11-12 level. He sounds like a man determined to put the worst possible interpretation on all the available data, rather than to take into account alternative explanations that paint a somewhat different picture. In particular, I intend to take issue with his interpretation of the results of international testing.

Let me begin, however, with some comments on the first part of his monograph, starting with the goals of education. While the first goal, training for earning a living, sounds good, Schweitzer should realize that a goal of this type would never be enunciated by teachers. Teachers believe that the goal of the school is to develop the intellectual, aesthetic, physical, emotional and ethical qualities of individuals.[1] These qualities may not sound very different from those goals stated by Schweitzer but there is still a profound difference in orientation. Earning a living, if it appeared in teachers' goals at all, would assume very secondary importance. It is interesting to note that the record of a poll given by Schweitzer in Table 5 confirms that teachers get the lowest grade on the dimension "preparation for working life." The finding is entirely consistent with the stated objectives of teachers.

Going on to the section on drop-outs, I must admit to some confusion. I have in my possession a document entitled *High School Non-Completion Rates: A Map of Current Measures*, prepared by the Education, Culture and Tourism Division of Statistics Canada.[2] This document indicates, on the basis of three different surveys, that the drop-out rate may be nearer to 18 percent than the 31 or 32 percent rate so often quoted. I am surprised, therefore, that Schweitzer does not quote that rate in his monograph, but refers to a 29 percent drop-out rate for boys and a 15 percent drop-out rate for girls. These figures do not seem to correspond to an overall rate of 18 percent.

Later on, he mentions an overall retention rate for the Canadian population of 63.3 percent. If he can introduce so much complexity into his figures, is it any wonder that the Canadian public may be quite confused as to the true drop-out and retention rates? He also refers to Hungary's superior performance on international tests as reducing Canada's advantage in terms of enrolment rates in upper secondary and tertiary education. But he does not mention that the enrolment rate for Canada is 30 points higher than the enrolment rate for Hungary. It seems to me that all Hungary's students would have to score 100 percent to overcome that sort of disadvantage.

Next Schweitzer considers the poll data from various surveys. What he does not mention, however, is that only a small minority of the population shows any real concern about the quality of Canadian education. This would seem to belie the opening statement, on page 1 of his monograph, that "parents are dissatisfied with the quality of schooling their children receive."

Then we come to the sections on testing. Schweitzer begins with an assessment of the results of several international tests of mathematics and science achievement conducted between 1980-1982 and 1990-91. He claims to have adjusted the scores to compensate for differences in years of schooling, drop-out rates and whether or not the subject was compulsory. However, it is not clear from the text just what adjustments were made. In any case, judging from the data as to rank given in Table 7, it is difficult to conclude that Canada does poorly, since in seven out of 10 tests of students aged nine to 14, Canada scored above the middle rank. It also ranked above the United States on all but one of the tests.

While the rank ordering of results is of some interest, it would be preferable to show the test results in the manner adopted by the OECD in its 1992 and 1993 reports, *Education at a Glance*.[3] This method consists of calculating the mean for each country, calculating the possible error in the data for each country resulting from the fact that the tests were administered only to a sample of students (the statistical error) and then comparing the mean scores among the participating countries while taking the standard error into account. When this method is followed, the results show that much of the supposed difference among countries is only a statistical artifact — i.e., that there is in fact no statistical significance in the difference in scores. Thus, in the results on the IEA tests of 13-year-olds (1982), there was found to be no statistical difference in the scores of Japan, Netherlands, Belgium, France and the two participating Canadian provinces. Similar results were obtained in a variety of other studies. Using these results instead of the data on ranking shows Canada consistently in the ranks of the top-scoring nations in these international tests.

Another problem with the international tests that has not yet been cleared up is the attribution of explanatory data. It stands to reason that two of the main factors that may contribute to the variation in marks among countries are the incidence of poverty in particular nations and the extent to which the implied curriculum of the international test represents the actual curriculum of each participating country. As to the incidence of poverty, no data have been forthcoming on the degree found in each nation, although it is well established in the various studies that socio-economic status has a considerable bearing on the results. And while detailed studies of curriculum accompany some of the international studies, no results have come out indicating how well students in various countries did on the curriculum content they had actually studied.

There is also some doubt as to the validity of the sampling in the international studies. Could some countries have tampered with the sampling by leaving out particular schools where scores would be low? It is impossible now to tell. But the extreme reverence paid to Japanese schools ought to be tempered by accounts of Japanese schools given by those who are natives of Japan. One such native is Kazuo Ishizaka, of the National Institute for Educational Research in Japan, who delivered a paper at a Canadian Teachers' Federation conference two years ago. Among other remarks he made the following. "I have been teaching mathematics for 10 years and I know very well how well they do. Their average for the intended curriculum was just around five points or less when I was a teacher of mathematics. That means the majority of Japanese high school students do not attain what is intended by the government."[4]

Schweitzer draws attention to the much lower rankings of results for 18 year-old students, a situation which is admittedly true. The explanation for the lower ranking is not hard to find. It arises from the fact that a much higher proportion of the population was included as mathematics specialists in the test. The general rule is that the larger the proportion of students included, the lower the scores. In the 1980-82 mathematics test, the proportion of the population classified as specialists was 30 percent in both the participating provinces (British Columbia and Ontario), whereas for other countries the proportions were 12 percent (Sweden and Japan), 11 percent (New Zealand) and six percent (England and Wales).[5]

Fortunately, Schweitzer concludes that emulation of the Japanese and Korean systems of education would not be suitable. He should perhaps have concluded that it would not be necessary either.

With regard to the interprovincial comparisons, one wonders why Schweitzer omitted the mathematics content questions, which were answered quite well, and focussed only on the problem-solving questions, which were not. In contrast to the wide variation in provincial differences to which Schweitzer refers, my reading is that most provinces got very similar results, with exceptions being the high results in Quebec and Manitoba French and the low results in Newfoundland, Prince Edward Island and the Northwest Territories. Unfortunately, there is only limited discussion of the reasons why such differences might be found. Certainly, it seems clear enough that the Manitoba French were mainly an immersion group and therefore probably above-average in attainment. With regard to Newfoundland, the results may owe a lot to the isolation of a proportion of the population sustained over many generations. In the Northwest Territories, the preponderance of the population is native, with a known impact on attainment levels. Among the other provinces there was little difference. In fact, an analysis of the type carried out for the OECD taking into account the standard error would probably demonstrate no statistically significant differences at all.

I would also like to call into question both the comparisons presented as part of the section on intertemporal comparisons. With regard to the data on CTBS results, my understanding is that this information was collected from the results of consecutive re-normings of the test. They were not designed for comparison of results over time, and there is no guarantee that the tests remained the same over time. Hence, use of the data to show changes over time may be questionable.

With regard to the supposed deterioration in literacy of the 16-24 year olds, this anomaly in data showing a general improvement in literacy over the generations has been much discussed. It is present not only in the Canadian data on literacy, but has also been found in US studies of literacy as well. One explanation advanced is that those in the 16-20 age group have not yet reached the peak of their functional literacy skill and still have a way to go. If this is indeed so, it might perhaps be appropriate to leave out this particular age group when reporting the data gleaned from future studies.

In his conclusion that the upgrading of apprenticeship programs is a necessity one may heartily concur. However, it seems that the Canadian context is not conducive to the development of a broad array of apprenticeship programs.

It is rather insulting, however, to have the remark about Japanese students being four years ahead of their American counterparts thrown in. In the first place, it should be remembered that Canadian students outperform American students on virtually every international test. Therefore, it should not be assumed that Canadians and Americans are identical. Furthermore, I feel that there is something wrong with these statements about Japanese students. To put it briefly, where are the students who score only five percent on their mathematics tests? I suspect that these students are not included in whatever population was used to establish this comparison.

In general, then, I question Schweitzer's conclusion that Canadian results are mediocre, that interprovincial differences are wide and that there has been no improvement over time. Rather, my reading of the data is that Canada scores in the top ranks of the industrialized nations, that interprovincial differences are in most cases fairly narrow and that there has been some improvement over time, but less pronounced improvement since education became truly universal after the Second World War.

Schweitzer's next suggestions all seem to make sense. For example, the possible detrimental effect of too much part-time work by high school students, the need to read to children and the possible effect of too much television viewing all seem worthy of consideration, as does the fact that socio-economic status plays a big role in achievement.

I would, however, take issue with his pronouncements on the teaching profession. While it appears to be true that people with lower scores are being attracted to teaching in the US, the same is not true for Canada. There is no indication in Canada at all that prospective teachers are being deterred from entering the profession, or that the applicants lack skills. On the contrary, there is a great excess of prospects over actual entrants, and as a consequence entry requirements have risen considerably.

With regard to the so-called shortness of the school year, I would suggest that misunderstandings have led to a belief that the Japanese school year is incredibly long compared with Canada's (243 days, compared with 185-190). It turns out that the Japanese school year is different in that students must attend for about one-third of a day on Saturdays. When that is translated into full-time equivalent school days it gives about 215, of which perhaps two weeks is devoted to such things as ceremonies and cleaning the school. In essence, then, the Japanese school year is no longer than the Canadian.

I would also call into question the supposed superiority of the Japanese primary school, again quoting from Kazuo Ishizaka. "Japan has no gifted and talented programs....so many of the Japanese kids bring small toys and hide them in their desk and are playing almost always."[6] That does not sound superior to Canadian schools, where an attempt is made to engage all students in activities suitable to their age and ability.

Further, Schweitzer says that a high school graduation diploma is not a guarantee of functional literacy. I would beg to differ with him. The survey of adult literacy undertaken by Statistics Canada in 1990 shows that 77 percent of high school graduates whose parents were English-speaking had acquired level 4 literacy and that a further 19 percent had level 3 literacy, thus leaving only about four percent in the illiterate categories. (Corresponding figures for graduates whose parents were French-speaking were 70 percent with level 4, 23 percent with level 3 and seven percent in lower categories.)[7]

Finally, I would note that the research proposal Schweitzer suggests on the influence of the home environment sounds very much like the longitudinal study of children, which is already under way under Statistics Canada auspices. The Canadian Teachers' Federation supports this study and wishes to add a stronger literacy component to it.

In conclusion, I would like to say that two people can read the same evidence and come up with different points of view. My reading of the evidence is that Canadian schools are doing a good job of preparing students for the future and are performing in the same league as most of their international competitors. There is undoubtedly room for improvement, however, and there Schweitzer and I can agree that substantial improvements in education can only be brought about with the full cooperation of all the agencies in society, and with the special intervention of the family. In fact, if the family could in all cases make the full contribution required to enhance the educational chances of the children, most of the other worries about the educational standing of Canadian children would fall away.

NOTES

1. Canadian Teachers' Federation, *Its Objectives, Its Policy* (Ottawa: CTF, 1992).

2. Education, Culture and Tourism Division, *High School Non-Completion Rates: A Map of Current Measures*, Statistics Canada, Ottawa, May 11, 1993.

3. Centre for Educational Research and Innovation, Organization for Economic Co-operation and Development, *Education at a Glance* (Paris: OECD, 1992-1993).

4. Kazuo Ishizaka, "Japanese Education: The Myths and The Realities," *Different Visions of the Future of Education*, Report of a conference, Canadian Teachers' Federation, Ottawa, May 2-5, 1993, p. 118.

5. David F. Robitaille, *Canadian Participation in the Second International Mathematics Study*, Working Paper No. 6 (Ottawa: Economic Council of Canada, 1990).

6. Ishizaka, "Japanese Education," pp. 120-21.

7. Labour and Household Survey Division, *Adult Literacy in Canada: Results of a National Study* (Ottawa: Statistics Canada, 1991).

A Response to Crocker and Gilliss

by

Thomas T. Schweitzer

T H O M A S   T .   S C H W E I T Z E R

A RESPONSE TO CROCKER AND GILLISS

Geraldine Gilliss' comments can be summarized as: there is nothing
wrong with the Canadian educational system, but whatever may be
wrong, it is anybody's fault except that of the educational establishment.
The lady doth protest too much, methinks. The readers will have to
decide whether it is I who have drawn a more balanced picture.

Gilliss "admit[s] to some confusion" about the section on drop-outs.
This is not surprising. Statistics Canada avoids the popular term "drop-
outs" and uses the term "non-completers." Furthermore, it publishes no
fewer than six concepts of non-completers, each differing in definition,
method and frequency of collection, and each having its own strengths
and weaknesses. The interested reader can find a good summary of these
points in the Statistics Canada publication quoted in my monograph.[1] In
any case, figures in isolation are not very useful; they become meaningful
only when compared in a valid manner with other figures. The 32 percent rate Gilliss complains about is arrived at by a method I outlined in
my monograph. It uses administrative data of the provincial departments of Education and provides more or less uninterrupted information
over 20-odd years. Gilliss' 18 percent comes from a one-time telephone
interview of a sample of 20 year-old adults and refers to them reporting

to have obtained a graduation certificate or else still continuing with their high school studies. The same telephone interview also surveyed 18 and 19 year-olds. Note that students who do not interrupt their studies or repeat grades would usually graduate by age 19 at the latest. The survey found that 31 percent of 19 year-olds reported not having graduated yet, but some may do so eventually. Thus the results from the two datasets are not really contradictory. For international comparisons probably the figure contained in Table 2 is the most useful one.

Only a philistine would regard training for earning a living as the chief or only purpose of education. But the ancient Roman who said that you must first make a living if you wish to devote yourself to the pursuit of wisdom was no philistine. Most Canadian parents and many students would agree with him, all the more because the knowledge, skills and working habits needed for earning a living are also indispensable prerequisites of the other educational goals emphasized by the teachers. If Canadian educators seriously object to the priorities of the parents, who have, after all, largely received their schooling in Canada, and who are now footing the bill for education of the next generation *via* their taxes, then I must conclude that they were not very successful in transmitting their values to their pupils.

I agree with Gilliss that we read the international test results differently. As for the 10 studies dealing with students aged nine to 14, their *cumulative* impact is one of mediocre achievement, even if individual test differences do not reach the (extremely high) statistical significance criteria adopted from the physical sciences. Inspecting the results, I find that in one study Canada just barely ranks among the top 25 percent of the participating countries, in another one it barely avoids ranking among the bottom 25 percent, and in the remaining eight we score in the broad middle range. This is no occasion for self-congratulation or even satisfaction. The situation becomes worse if we subdivide the 10 studies into the five conducted in the 1980s and the other five in the 1990s. In the 1980s, on the average, 35 percent of the participating countries did better than Canada and 65 percent did worse. In the 1990s, 52 percent of the other countries did better than we and 48 percent did worse. Are we slipping? Our teachers rightly complain that the students could do better but have no ambition to do so. Reading the remarks of the Director of Research and Information Services of the Canadian Teachers' Federation I am wondering about the example the teachers are setting.

Coming to the test results of the 18 year-old students, Gilliss points out that we have a relatively high retention rate in high school, and this low selectivity reduces our average achievement. This is correct as far as it goes, but there is more to the problem. In this age group only those students were tested who took at least five hours of mathematics instruction per week, or advanced level science courses in the last year of high school. In our high schools a student can graduate without taking mathematics or science in the last year of school. It is well known that only those students are taking these subjects who are relatively strong in them. Elective subjects are much rarer in most European countries: a student must take math and science in the last year of high school, whether one likes it or not. Here the selectivity works in favour of Canada (and the United States and England). However, the answer is *not* that valid international comparisons are not possible at this age group. I wish to draw the attention of the technically minded reader to the adjusting technique cited in this monograph.[2] It shows that our 18 year-old students do not do well in the tested subjects. Perhaps this is not surprising. As Table 7 line 4 shows, at age 14, when education is general and compulsory in all advanced countries and electivity of mathematics is as yet non-existent, Japan is already way ahead of Canada. The same Kazuo Ishizaka whom Gilliss also quotes told me in private conversation and correspondence that there is very little difference in the (very high) achievement among Japanese students up to the end of primary schooling. Some differences show up by the end of the lower secondary, and the differences become very big by the end of the extremely selective and demanding higher secondary education. It is the very thorough general foundation of basic skills at the lower levels that enables the strongest students to become champions later on.

Gilliss suggests that our mediocre showing in the international tests may be due to "the incidence of poverty." It is quite true that scholastic achievement of students is highly correlated with the socio-economic status of their families. However Canada is still one of the richest countries in the world — we are ranking fifth among the 24 nations of the OECD. It is hard to believe that our mediocre showing is due to poverty. On the other hand, if our students continue with this unimpressive level of achievement, the income and standard of living of the next generations may well sink to that of the average industrialized countries.

It is also true that students' test results depend on whether they have been taught the material that is being tested. That is why it is so disquieting to find that the Canadian curriculum is relatively impoverished compared to those of most leading European countries. This has been strikingly demonstrated in various studies, including the one by the Alberta Chamber of Resources, published by Alberta Education and cited in my monograph.[3]

Regarding the SAIP interprovincial test in mathematics, I reported the results of problem solving, because teachers often complain that tests deal only with lower-order skills. The results of the lower skill "content knowledge" test was very similar to the problem-solving part. For instance in content knowledge, Ontario (English) is almost two years behind Quebec (French) and the difference between the strongest and weakest system is close to five years! To maintain that such differences are minor, and do not matter, is, to say the least, surprising.

As for the Canadian Test of Basic Skills (CTBS), Geraldine Gilliss is in error. At the time of recalibration, Nelson Canada performed the necessary tests to make intertemporal comparisons possible and valid.

Concerning the Statistics Canada test of functional literacy, and her explanation that the 16-20 age group has not yet reached the peak of its functional literacy skill, I must suspect that she never read the test questions. They are so simple and straightforward that if a person has reading problems with that material at the age of 16, he or she will have problems with it at whatever age. Gilliss expresses satisfaction that 71 percent of 16 to 24 year-olds reached Level 4 achievement, 23 percent Level 3, and only six percent Levels 1 and 2. Perhaps she has not read the fine print defining Level 3. It says: "Canadians at this level can use reading materials in a variety of situations *provided the material is simple, clearly laid out and the tasks involved are not too complex.* While these people generally do not see themselves as having major reading difficulties, *they tend to avoid situations requiring reading.*" (my emphasis.) I question whether those 29 percent who do not reach Level 4 will be able to function well in the working life of the 21st century; even less will they be able to reach those educational goals to which Gilliss, the Canadian teachers and I too assign higher priorities.

Regarding functional numeracy, the situation is even worse. In this sub-test, those surveyed were classified into three levels. Level 3 is defined as follows: "Canadians at this level can deal with material requiring them to perform simple sequences of numerical operations which enable them to meet most everyday demands." At Level 2, they "can deal with material requiring them to perform a simple numerical operation such as an addition or subtraction." Statistics Canada found that 44 percent of 16-24 year-olds did not reach Level 3 and thus were *not* able "to meet most everyday demands."

Finally, Geraldine Gilliss thinks that the Statistics Canada longitudinal survey will answer most of the questions mentioned in my proposed research study. I wish it were so. The Statistics Canada survey deals with the health and welfare questions of Canadian children — a worthy and highly important area of inquiry — for which Statistics Canada is to be commended. However, the study deals only tangentially with questions of education, not in the breath and depth this subject requires.

Many of the points raised by Crocker I have already answered in my rejoinder to Gilliss. Here I will respond to some additional questions.

A thorough discussion of the state of Canadian education would require a hefty tome rather than a modest monograph. Given the present format, judgment in the selection of material and simplification of presentation is unavoidable.

I think there is less disagreement between Crocker and me than his remarks seem to imply. For instance, I fully share his view about the overwhelming importance of motivation and effort, and of the great influence of the home environment on educational achievement. Nor do we disagree on the need for, and the possibility of, raising the *general* level of achievement in the first eight years of schooling, and on the importance of the effective use of time in school. Also, I agree with him on the deleterious effect of television, but I cannot dismiss the effect of work for pay as easily as he does, when findings show that, even among Ontario male high school graduates, 34 percent worked 20 hours or more per week in their last year of schooling.

We also agree that public opinion polls have to be treated with caution; even those sponsored by the Canadian Education Association. Therefore I find it surprising that Crocker recommends the use of such polls for determining the goals of education. As for using the "mission statements" of provincial governments, most of these are disturbingly vague and unspecific. The quoted example of British Columbia is a case in point. By contrast, the goal of Newfoundland is refreshingly specific, but, unfortunately, not typical.

I disagree with Crocker's opinion that economists have not turned their attention seriously to the debate between the productivity increasing and the screening hypotheses of education. To mention just one example: *Economics of Education: Research and Studies* contains in the section on Education and Employment 12 review articles with 193 references of books and articles, and in the section on Ability and Screening eight review articles with 105 references.[4] Few economists accept either hypothesis in its extreme form, and most agree that both hypotheses have some truth in them. But hardly any economist denies that education increases productivity, particularly so at the primary and secondary level.

I question Crocker's interpretation of Table 2 and his conclusion that "the drop-out problem in Canada can be solved simply by aligning the legal school living age with the age needed to attain the final year of secondary schooling." Observe that the full-time enrolment rate at age 17 in Canada, where secondary education is free, is 79.3 percent, while in Japan it is 88.8 percent, even though the latter country charges a stiff tuition fee for senior high school tuition. This tells us quite a lot about the attitude of the schools, students, parents and society in general toward education in the respective countries.

A hasty reader of Crocker's comments would think that I claimed that "...decreasing class size by, say, one-third would yield an increase of 50 to 100 percent in costs." What I said was: "...a reduction of the class size by one third *to one half*...implies an increase in schooling costs of *close to* 50 to 100 percent." It is quite true that certain educational costs are fixed, but we must not forget that halving the class size implies not only a doubling of the number of teachers in the classrooms, but also of the number of needed classrooms and of certain kinds of classroom equipment.

Crocker questions whether "administrative inputs have a detrimental effect on achievement." Yet in his next paragraph he points out that "it is possible to find classes as large as 35 in Newfoundland schools, despite the existence of a 15:1 pupil/teacher ratio. Significant reductions in class size could be achieved with no additional personnel if more teachers were deployed to classroom duties, rather than to other work." Presumably this other work is of an administrative nature, which thus diverts resources from classroom teaching.

Crocker maintains that "this monograph conveys a highly pessimistic view of the state of education in Canada." Yet, I think, ultimately it is Crocker who is more pessimistic than I. It is he who says that "[i]t is by no means certain that Canadian society is ready to take additional time from other activities in pursuit of higher achievement." While I agree with him that we must strive to "educate children to an established [higher] standard of achievement," I question that we must "change from the basic premise that the goal of education is to educate children to the limits of their ability." Such a change implies the imposition of a "Robin Hood approach" to schooling: i.e., helping one group of students at the expense of some other group. Quite apart from the fact that educational research in its present state cannot tell us how much more or fewer resources it would take to raise the achievement level at one end of the ability scale than at the other, the social sciences cannot tell the short- and long-term consequences of, say, raising the achievement level of the weakest 10 percent of students by five percentage points at the cost of lowering the achievement of the top 10 percent of students by the corresponding amount. However, I do not think that we must follow the Robin Hood approach. In our cities, at least, there is no reason why three or four neighbouring high schools could not co-operate to set aside at least one class per subject and grade for a curriculum aimed at the very strongest students. Such an approach would imply for many students a 20-30 minute trip each way on public transportation, but this is not unacceptable at high school age. While the other schools would lose some of their very strongest students, they would retain that nucleus of at least average level students which is, according to the literature of effective schools, the precondition of good education.

N o t e s

1. Sid Gilbert, L. Barr, W. Clark, M. Blue and D. Sunter, *Leaving School: Results from a National Survey Comparing School Leavers and High School Graduates 18 to 20 Years of Age* (Ottawa: Minister of Supply and Services, 1993).
2. Thomas T. Schweitzer, *International and Interprovincial Comparisons of Student Cognitive Achievement,* Working Paper No. 39 (Ottawa: Economic Council of Canada,1992).
3. Alberta Chamber of Resources, *International Comparisons in Education: Curriculum, Values and Lessons* (Edmonton: Alberta Education, 1992).
4. George Psacharapoulos (ed.), *Economics of Education: Research and Studies* (Oxford: Pergamon Press, 1987).

Thomas T. Schweitzer was born in Hungary and received his Doctorate in Economic Science from the University of Technology and Economic Science in Budapest in 1948. He arrived in Canada in 1953 and was Senior Economist with the Economic Council of Canada from 1964 to 1992. He is now an independent economic consultant. Among his publications are: "The Issue of Quality" in *Education and Training in Canada: A Research Report*; *International and Interprovincial Comparisons of Student Cognitive Achievement*; *Schooling and the Statistics Canada Survey of Literacy Skills Used in Daily Activities*; and "Collective Bargaining, Teachers, and Student Achievement: a Comment" in the *Journal of Labour Research*.

Robert Crocker holds an honours degree in Physics and a B.Ed. degree from Memorial University and a Ph.D. in science education from the University of Alberta. He has been a member of the Faculty of Education at Memorial University since 1969. He was Dean of the Faculty of Education from 1990 to 1993. Since 1993, he has been on secondment as Associate Deputy Minister of Education for Newfoundland. He has written extensively, both books and articles, on science education, curriculum and classroom teaching, and acts as a consultant on various aspects of education. In his current position, he is responsible for implementing the report of the 1992 Royal Commission on Education.

Geraldine Gilliss is a native of Ottawa, Ontario, and received her education at Carleton University and the University of Toronto. She has been employed by the Canadian Teachers' Federation since 1957 and currently holds the position of Director of Research and Information Services. Mrs. Gilliss has particular responsibility at the Federation for analysis, interpretation and conduct of research in the interrelated areas of teacher education, teacher evaluation and teacher and school effectiveness. Over the past year, she has been engaged in continuing study in areas such as disadvantaged children, teacher and school effectiveness, teacher education and teacher evaluation.

Stephen T. Easton (series editor) is Professor of Economics at Simon Fraser University. He received his Ph.D. from the University of Chicago in 1978. In addition to his *Education in Canada* (1988), he has written extensively in the fields of international economics and economic history. Professor Easton has been on the editorial board of the *Canadian Journal of Economics* and has served as associate editor for *Economic Inquiry*.

RECENT IRPP PUBLICATIONS

EDUCATION:
Stephen B. Lawton, *Busting Bureaucracy to Reclaim our Schools*
Bruce Wilkinson, *Educational Choice: Necessary But Not Sufficient*
Peter Coleman, *Learning About Schools: What Parents Need to Know and How They Can Find Out*
Edwin G. West, *Ending the Squeeze on Universities*

GOVERNANCE:
Peter Aucoin, *The New Public Management: Canada in Comparative Perspective*
F. Leslie Seidle, *Rethinking the Delivery of Public Services to Citizens*
Kirk Cameron and Graham White, *Northern Governments in Transition: Political and Constitutional Development in the Yukon, Nunavut and the Western Northwest Territories*
G. Bruce Doern, *The Road to Better Public Services: Progress and Constraints in Five Canadian Federal Agencies*
Donald G. Lenihan, Gordon Robertson and Roger Tassé, *Canada: Reclaiming the Middle Ground*
F. Leslie Seidle (ed.), *Seeking a New Canadian Partnership: Asymmetrical and Confederal Options*
F. Leslie Seidle (ed.), *Equity and Community: The Charter, Interest Advocacy and Representation*
F. Leslie Seidle (ed.), *Rethinking Government: Reform or Reinvention?*

TELECOMMUNICATIONS:
W.T. Stanbury (ed.), *Perspectives on the New Economics and Regulation of Telecommunications*
Yves Rabeau, *Les télécommunications: problématique d'une industrie en évolution rapide*
Charles Sirois and Claude E. Forget, *The Medium and the Muse: Culture, Telecommunications and the Information Highway*
Charles Sirois et Claude E. Forget, *Le Médium et les Muses : la culture, les télécommunications et l'autoroute de l'information*

SOCIAL POLICY:
Adil Sayeed (ed.), *Workfare: Does it Work? Is it Fair?*
Monique Jérôme-Forget, Joseph White and Joshua M. Wiener (eds.), *Health Care Reform Through Internal Markets: Experience and Proposals*
Ross Finnie, *Child Support: The Guideline Options*
Elisabeth B. Reynolds (ed.), *Income Security: Changing Needs, Changing Means*
Jean-Michel Cousineau, *La Pauvreté et l'État: Pour un nouveau partage des compétences en matière de sécurité sociale*

CITY-REGIONS:
Andrew Sancton, *Governing Canada's City-Regions: Adapting Form to Function*
William Coffey, *The Evolution of Canada's Metropolitan Economies*

PUBLIC FINANCE:
Paul A.R. Hobson and France St-Hilaire, *Toward Sustainable Federalism: Reforming Federal-Provincial Fiscal Arrangements*

Choices\Choix

Social Security Reform:
The IRPP Position / IRPP prend position
Commentaries on the Axworthy Green Paper
Public Finance:
Restoring Generational Balance in Canada
Regional Distribution of Federal Corporate Tax Expenditures
Répartition régionale des dépenses fiscales touchant les corporations
À qui profitent les avantages fiscaux?
Health:
Les marchés internes dans le contexte canadien
Série Québec-Canada:
Un Québec souverain et l'union économique Québec-Canada
L'évolution du fédéralisme canadien
La monnaie d'un Québec souverain
The Future of the Anglophone Community in Québec/L'avenir de la communauté anglophone au Québec

Les peuples autochtones et l'avenir du Québec
Les implications économiques d'un Québec souverain
L'accession du Québec à la souveraineté: aspects juridiques

These and other publications are available from:
Renouf Publishing
1294 Algoma Road
Ottawa, Ontario
K1B 3W8
Tel.: (613) 741-4333
Fax: (613) 741-5439